DRIVEN CRAZY

Also by Leslie Scrase:

Days in the Sun (children's stories, with Jean Head)
In Travellings Often
Booklet on Anglican/Methodist Conversations
Some Sussex and Surrey Scrases
Diamond Parents
The Sunlight Glances Through (poetry)
Some Ancestors of Humanism
An Evacuee
Conversations (on Matthew's Gospel)
        between an Atheist and a Christian
A Prized Pupil!
A Reluctant Seaman
The Game Goes On (poetry)
It's Another World
A Talented Bureaucrat
Town Mouse and Country Mouse (nature diary)
More from the Country Mouse (nature diary)
Kenneth and Bob (children's story)
Coping With Death (three editions published)
Letting off Steam (short essays)
Scribblings of an old romantic (poems)
Happy Endings (short stories)
An Unbeliever's Guide to the Bible
The Four Gospels Through an Outside Window
        – A Commentary
Autobiography of a Blockhead (poetry)
Postscript (poetry)
Belief, Unbelief, Ethics and Life

Driven Crazy

My Life With Cars & Other Vehicles

LESLIE SCRASE

UNITED WRITERS
Cornwall

UNITED WRITERS PUBLICATIONS LTD
Ailsa, Castle Gate, Penzance, Cornwall.
www.unitedwriters.co.uk

British Library Cataloguing in Publication Data:
A catalogue record for this book is
available from the British Library.

ISBN 9781852001797

Printed and bound in Great Britain by
United Writers Publications Ltd.,
Cornwall.

To Wendy
who has endured so much
and enjoyed a little
thanks to my life with cars.

Acknowledgements

Recently my publisher, Malcolm Sheppard, told me that we have something in common: a love for the old Jaguar 4.2 and for VW Camper Vans. He also has something in common with my wife! Both of them hate it when I try to tell them how wonderful they are.

I was reading a book of Seneca's Letters published by Penguin recently and it struck me that Malcolm would never have allowed so many mistakes to be printed in a book he published. The manuscript of this book was even more of a mess than most of mine. I'm so grateful for his diligence and also for his encouragement over many years. He has been a true friend.

Contents

'though I deliver up these papers to the press,
I invite no man to the reading of them: and,
whosoever reads, and repents; it is his own fault,
I made this composition principally for myself.'

Sir Roger L'Estrange – 1673

Preface

DRIVEN crazy? Hasn't Les always been a bit loopy?

Well yes, I suppose he has. What was that quote from *Alice in Wonderland* that his brother Aubs was always spouting?

It was when Alice was asking directions from the Cheshire Cat. The Cat told her that she could either visit the Mad Hatter or the equally mad March Hare and Alice said that she didn't want to go among mad people.

"Oh, you can't help that," said the Cat: "we're all mad here. I'm mad. You're mad."

"How do you know I'm mad?" said Alice.

"You must be," said the Cat, "or you wouldn't have come here."

But although Alice was not convinced with this logic, those of you who know Les may well be. As I said, he's always been a bit on the loopy side. Take this book for example.

This book began as an account of my love affair with

cars. But then, like Topsy, it sort of grew and spread out in a number of different directions. But cars are still at the heart of it.

I once told a girlfriend of mine that whenever I was bored I bought a new car! There was SOME truth in that statement but it ceased to be true when I ran my own business. Then cars became an absolute necessity and they did such a mileage that they needed to be replaced fairly often – and as business grew, they needed to be added to.

But, looking back, I'm surprised at the number of vehicles we've had since we retired to Dorset. I have still NEEDED a car, of course, because I have gone on working. But one day we shall find ourselves driving our very last car. My dad gave up driving when he was 86 and I bought his car off him. But I was still perfectly happy to be a passenger when he was driving. So what about Wendy and me? When will we give up? After all, we are both in our 80s now. I still FEEL perfectly competent behind the wheel and I'm still working as a celebrant, so I need to drive, although I'm down to about 10,000 miles a year now. My mother used to say, "All unknown the future lies. Let it rest."

One way or another the day will come, and it may well be that we are on our last car already. Wendy loves it so much that she hopes so!

If we are, then perhaps this is the right time to write the story of my love affair with cars, in the hope that it may give some amusement and pleasure.

I have also taken the liberty of doing a bit of re-cycling from two of my earlier books: *Happy Endings* and *It's Another World*. Both are out of print now. I have a few copies of the second one left and it is still available in some libraries.

1

An Austin 16 and a
Green and Black Vauxhall

By the time I was born ours was a sizeable family, for I
had three elder brothers (my sister was to arrive later). My
father already had a car, an Austin 16. Because I grew up
knowing nothing else, it never crossed my mind that it was
unusual to grow up in a family with a car. After all, some
of my father's friends had cars too and one of my uncles
had a car that fairly often seemed to be tied up with string.

What is more, my father provided his parents with a
green and black Vauxhall and a chauffeur: Dimmock. I can
remember asking Dimmock what he did when he was just
waiting, never dreaming that the day would come when I
would do an awful lot of waiting for my own passengers.
He watched people. I went for long walks or sat reading –
even sleeping!

That Vauxhall had a number plate that would be worth
a small fortune nowadays: HMG 1. I did sometimes
wonder why my grandparents had the Vauxhall – in my
eyes the better car – and we only had the Austin.

Driving with my Dad was one of the great pleasures of my childhood. Although he didn't dawdle, he was not a fast driver. When people went tearing past us he would say, "There goes another one in a hurry to meet his accident." Or, if we were on a long journey, he would tell me to make a note of it. Fifty miles further on, with some sort of brief hold up – perhaps due to road works – he would point to the queue of cars ahead. Sure enough, three or four cars into the queue we would see the car that had gone haring past us. "That's where all his speed has got him," my Dad would say contentedly.

It was also on those long journeys that I first learned to read a map. Dad always obtained a route map from the AA before we set out and Mother would have it on her lap.

"Where next?" Dad would ask, and Mother would have her finger on the place where she had last given him instructions so she could tell him.

The trouble was, she often fell asleep in the front seat, so we might well have left the place where her finger was miles before. So I took to following our route on a map so that I could give Dad the correct instructions when Mother had been sleeping. And I cherished her voice from the front saying:

"You're a good boy."

It was so rare that anybody ever said that, or could do!

Dad was always steady and reliable. Passengers were never thrown about but felt comfortable and safe. I never knew him to be in a hurry. He loved to drive through the Sussex countryside and I came to love that kind of driving too. But perhaps my favourite times were those rare occasions when we had been to London to a show and drove home late at night. Happy and contented and a little bit sleepy, those journeys were magical.

When the war came Dad gave up his cars and, amongst other things, used part of his factory to store food stocks for the government. He used to examine those stocks regularly and one day discovered that two tins – I think of sardines – were damaged. He phoned up the ministry and asked if he should get rid of them.

"No, certainly not. We'll see to that."

So they did. They sent a lorry from London, ten miles away, to collect the two tins. I suspect that my dad wondered why he had bothered to give up his cars.

A few of my memories of driving with my dad date from before the war, but not many. Opposite our house there were some allotments and Dad kept our car in sheds behind the allotments. I can remember sitting on his lap and steering as we came from the allotments to the road.

And there was a trip to Box Hill from our home in East Croydon. When we got there we found a 'Stop me and Buy One' Wall's Ice Cream van. The chap selling ices had a row of medals across his chest. My brother Brian had a lovely singing voice and had won medals for his singing, so naturally I said to my dad: "*He* must have a good singing voice!"

There were the journeys on holiday, often to Felpham near Bognor. My two eldest brothers would set off on their bikes after breakfast. The rest of us didn't get away until about 11.00am, all packed into the Austin 16. For miles my mother would be wondering, "Did I close the windows?"; "Did I turn off the gas?" – you know the sort of thing. But before we left, my third brother, Aubs, would take me around the house checking, and then in the car we could take turns saying, "Yes, Mother," until she was finally able to relax.

After the war Dad brought the same car back into use but we moved house into the Surrey countryside. It is from that period that my memories of driving home at night from London come. I can also remember quite a lot of individual memories, including one when he drove me from his office in Croydon to our house. We were almost home when he suddenly said, "I've forgotten your mother." She was in Croydon playing bridge, so back we went and I was instructed not to say a word.

My two greatest memories of those years and the Austin were of chains on the wheels in the winter of 1947, one of the coldest winters of the century, and of driving in the fog. Cars in those days still had running boards – a step outside the doors, presumably to make getting in and out of a car more elegant for the ladies! Dad would crawl along through the country lanes with his driver's window down and with me standing on the running board shouting instructions.

People find it almost impossible to believe nowadays, but in the thickest fogs it really was true that you could stretch your hand out in front of you and not be able to see it. Once, when I had an Austin of my own, I drove straight across a T junction and into a hedge. Fortunately the hedge had the signpost I needed to guide me the rest of the way!

Anyway, with all my experiences of my father's driving, it was no wonder that, as I grew older, I always wanted a car of my own.

Before I leave those childhood days, let me mention my amateur survey. It would have been the late 1940s: 1947/8? We went on holiday to Newquay and I decided to make a note of the makes of all the cars I saw. Over 70% of them were made by Austin and about another 20% Morris. Most of the rest were Fords, with just a tiny percentage of Standards, Hillmans, Vauxhalls and so on. Except for the American giants Ford and General Motors (Vauxhall), they are all gone now. It hardly seems possible that the British car industry could collapse so completely, but it has.

It was while I was in the Navy that I learned to drive. My boss used to send me ashore once a week on 'escort duties'. It was my girlfriend's half-day! I would have my lesson in a Morris 8 with the British School of Motoring and then spend the afternoon with my girl. When it came to my test, my instructor said, "If you get Mr A or Mr B, you'll pass but Mr C will fail you." I didn't know it until afterwards but I got Mr C.

All went well until we met a bus coming down a narrow lane. I carefully took to the pavement and congratulated myself on keeping calm and doing it so well. FAILED! If I met a bus on that lane today I would do the same thing, but I should have reversed all the way down the lane. Never mind. Three more lessons and I received my driving licence – the most important qualification of my life.

2

Preparing the Way

I need to prepare the way a bit before I tell you about my first car. I don't think I would have bought it at all but for my motorbike.

I was a student at Richmond College in Surrey and my girlfriend was in Plymouth, so I decided to buy a motorbike. As another student had experience of bikes, we went together to look around and bought an ex-war department 350cc Royal Enfield. He showed me how to ride it and I rode three times round Richmond Park with him on the back.

The following weekend, with a dusting of snow on the ground, I rode to Plymouth wearing my eldest brother's old flying suit which only partly kept out the cold. Goodness knows how cold he must have got flying in Mosquitos over to Germany and back.

By the time I got to Exeter I was so cold that I couldn't change gear with my foot. Instead I had to bend down and move the gear lever with my hand, and by the time I got to Plymouth I wasn't even strong enough to put the bike on its stand! I thought at least I was guaranteed a sympathetic welcome... but my girlfriend and her dad opened the front door and just stood there hooting with laughter!

Usually I don't find it too difficult to laugh at myself. After all, there are plenty of occasions when I'm the most colossal idiot. But on that occasion, like Queen Victoria, I 'was not amused'.

However, idiocy marked my next experience. This was on an occasion when I was making the same trip and Exeter featured once more – it will feature fairly frequently in the pages ahead.

My exhaust fell off. So I stopped, put the bike on its stand and went back and picked up the exhaust – and dropped it pretty quickly! I don't need to tell you, of course, that it was rather hot. But as so often in my life, I got lucky. An AA chap came along on his bike and side-car and I was able to wave him down.

Could he help me? Not unless I was a member. So I became a member on the spot and he put my exhaust back on.

Although I used the bike a lot I was never a 'biker'. I didn't really enjoy biking and, even when I managed to push it up to 52 mph (downhill), I didn't find that I was excited by speed. So when I started it up at college one day and it caught fire, I just stood well back and looked forward to the insurance money. But unfortunately I hadn't bargained on a student friend of mine, Alf Lawson, who came rushing out of college with a fire extinguisher and put the fire out. So I was stuck with my bike; but not for all that long.

One summer's day I was down in Cornwall and came off the bike on a steep hill near Liskeard, landing on my head. But for the protection of my woolly pom-pom hat goodness knows what damage might have been done. As it was I spent a week in Liskeard Cottage Hospital being wonderfully well looked after. I wasn't the first to come off on that hill, and after my accident it was finally decided that the road was suffering too much damage, so a warning notice was put up telling drivers of the danger.

At everyone's insistence I parted company with my motorbike forever. In fact, the only other motorbike I ever had was lent me by a Naval Officer on a six months' tour of the Mediterranean. He had a 250cc BSA Bantam. I rode it all over the place (I was a young minister at the time) and finally seized it up on my way home from Dartmoor just two weeks before he was due home! I had it repaired, told him and he laughed.

"You shouldn't have bothered. I could have repaired that. It would have given me something to do while I'm on leave."

But, to go back to my own bike. As soon as it had gone I found myself beginning to look at cars! I was tempted by a hopelessly unsuitable big Alvis sports car, but even I managed to be sensible and not buy it.

Meanwhile I got to know a young American couple who were on their way back to the States. While here they owned a Hillman Minx and spent money on it to ensure that it was in really good condition. I made the mistake of writing to my dad to tell him that I was thinking of buying it. He wrote me a long letter back (he was very good at writing long letters) in which he pointed out all the defects of Hillmans and warned me against buying it. So I didn't.

I was so naïve – just how naïve will appear in due course. It never entered my head that my dad would have written a very similar letter no matter what car I wanted to buy. He just didn't want me to buy a car at all. I was still a student, after all. To him the idea of me having a car was just folly. He was right, of course – but it meant that I missed the chance of buying a nice little car in excellent condition.

Which brings us at last to the story of the car I did buy. I had been thumbing lifts from London to Plymouth and as evening came on I had just left Exeter behind. A sports car pulled up. I jumped into what little space there was in the back and the two men in the car took me at great speed the rest of the way to Plymouth.

Was it the next day that I found myself at a garage looking at cars? Blow me if those two men didn't come out to speak to me! Before long I found myself the proud owner of (although I didn't know it) a crap Austin 7 of 1934 vintage. 'Crap' is perhaps unfair. After one or two adventures it became a very reliable little car. It cost me £70.

One of my newfound friends turned the starting handle and the engine burst into life. I leapt out of the forecourt of the garage and promptly broke a half-shaft. My friends repaired it free of charge and I set off again, kangaroo-jumping across Plymouth. No one from the British School of Motoring had needed or bothered to teach me that on old cars you had to double-de-clutch every time you changed gear.

Once double-de-clutching was no longer double-de-Dutch to me, I was ready for the open road. My love affair with cars was about to begin. And although cars are, of course, feminine, I named mine after my brother Aubrey, and the story of Aubrey the Austin can now begin in earnest.

3

Aubrey the Austin

Now that I knew how to drive him, we were free to enjoy the open road, and back in the 1950s the roads were still largely empty, especially on places like Dartmoor.

I was happily trundling along a side road on Dartmoor. A long, steep, winding road stretched out before me. Perhaps I had better drop down a gear? And that was when I broke a half shaft again, and when I discovered that my brakes were virtually non-existent!

We rattled and bumped and bounced fast and faster down the winding hill. We just managed to turn enough to get over the little bridge at the bottom of the hill and then our momentum carried us part way up the other side until at last we stopped – briefly. But then we began to roll backwards!

Fortunately there was a side path leading up through grass to a gate into a field. I was able to reverse onto the path, and the grass and mud were sufficient to hold the car still when it finally stopped.

It was a long walk to the nearest garage but the repairs

they carried out proved to be enough to turn Aubrey into a very reliable friend for the rest of our time together.

So my journey back to college in Surrey passed without incident. This was the life. No more thumbing for lifts for me.

But of course, every so often cars need petrol. A few days later I stopped at a garage near the level crossing in East Sheen and a man came out and filled Aubrey up.

"Do you require oil and water, sir?"

Oil and water? I hadn't a clue. Did cars need oil and water as well as petrol? So I said, "I don't know."

"Perhaps you would like me to check, sir?"

"Yes please." I felt a right prat, a bit like Bertie Wooster. I didn't even know how to open the bonnet. But the man did.

He opened it up and showed me the dip stick and how to check my oil. I needed rather a lot on this occasion! He showed me where to put the oil and then showed me the car's radiator. I needed quite a lot of water, too.

"Perhaps we ought to check the battery while we are about it."

He showed me the battery and told me that we used distilled water for that – and yes, the battery needed topping up as well.

"And what about your tyres sir, shall we just have a look at those?"

I was now on familiar territory. I knew about tyres but we checked them all the same. And then we walked to his little cubby hole for me to pay. He took my money and thanked me, adding: "It's quite a good idea to check all those things on your car once a week, sir."

Never by the slightest hint of a smile or by the

snootiness of superior knowledge did he give the glimmer of a sign that he felt that I was the most naïve twit he had ever met in his life. But in those few brief moments he had taught me almost all that I have ever known about the inner workings of cars and their maintenance. I learned how to use a grease gun on my own!

It was not long after this that I was off back down to the West Country again. By now I was familiar with almost everything on the car, although there was a small light-switch on the steering column that didn't seem to do anything at all.

It was a dark and stormy night as I drove over Dartmoor once more. My headlights were virtually useless, especially when I was driving uphill because the harder the engine had to work, the slower the windscreen wipers went – almost to the point of stopping completely. Windscreen wipers on old cars used to do that. It made life very difficult when the weather was as foul as it was that night. I leaned forward to clear the inside of the windscreen and that was when, quite by accident, I hit the light switch on my steering column. And then I discovered what it was for. Suddenly my headlights became mildly useful as they changed from dipped to full beams and with nobody else on the road, I never needed to dip them again.

Our next bit of excitement was back in London – a typical bit of student stupidity.

A visiting football team had seen the portrait of a man who had been one of our lecturers and who was now one of their lecturers. So they 'borrowed' it. For a while no one noticed, but when we did we were irate. Two of us had cars. I had Aubrey and another student had a Morris 8 sports car. Being a sports car, he could go faster than I could. I could get about 30 mph out of Aubrey. He could get 35 out of his!

Two car loads of students set off across north London, but in the end it only needed two of us. It was easy enough to climb through a downstairs window while one of our students (dressed as a police constable) strolled up and down in front of their college. We recovered our portrait and took one or two extra trophies as well. And then it was decided that our two cars should race back to college.

By faithfully ignoring every set of traffic lights in those early hours of the morning, Aubrey managed to keep in front all the way to Richmond, only to be pippcd to the entrance of our college drive.

A couple of weeks later the students voted to return our trophies to their rightful home, but two of us felt that all of our work as thieves deserved better, so we hid the trophies and they were not returncd until the end of term.

I have two other insignificant memories – perhaps both of them from the same journey; I'm not sure. Both memories are associated with journeys from Plymouth to Surrey. After travelling from Plymouth to Honiton, to the east of Honiton there is a long, long hill. Today you would hardly notice it but back then many vehicles found it hard work and Aubrey was no exception.

We had just begun to climb the hill when we found ourselves at the back of a considerable army convoy with a lot of lorry-loads of troops. When they saw my girl-friend in the passenger seat you can imagine the sort of reactions we got. Slowly and laboriously I managed to persuade Aubrey to overtake one vehicle at a time until at last, almost at the top of the hill, we were free of them all. And that is when the radiator boiled over!

25

b

We pulled into the side of the road. If we had had ribald comments before, you can imagine what they were now. In due course we carried on, bought some petrol and put water in the radiator. After a fair drive we climbed up onto the Hog's Back in Surrey. By now there was a fair wind blowing and it was tipping down with rain. As we began to drop down towards Guildford I found it virtually impossible to keep the car on the left hand side of the road. At every bend in the road curving towards the left, Aubrey would drift across to the right. Fortunately there was no oncoming traffic!

For a long time after that Aubrey and I travelled happily together without incident – until I spent a weekend with a friend who lived in Newmarket.

We had driven from Newmarket to see Ely Cathedral. As we were driving home I came out from a minor road onto a major road and turned left. A learner driver was coming down the major road behind me – rather faster than I realised. He didn't slow. He didn't adjust his steering to overtake me. He just panicked and drove straight into the back of me sending me off the road into a ditch where we rested in long grass. I sat there hooting with laughter, but my companion was not amused!

There wasn't much damage done except for a pierced petrol tank. With help, we managed to push the car back onto the road and had just enough petrol to get us to a garage where they repaired the tank.

At the end of the weekend I drove back to London straight down the A1. I even managed to overtake a lorry or two. There were traffic lights where the A1 crosses the north circular road. I waited for them to turn green and then turned right, failing to notice a car bearing down on

26

me. It was going straight across the north circular and ploughed into me. I don't remember much of what happened after that. Poor Aubrey was sold for scrap. I returned to college after a trip to hospital.

As I walked into college with my head wrapped up in bandages and my right arm in a sling I met the Principal.

"How *are* you, Mr Scrase?"

"Very well, thank you, sir."

"I don't think you are VERY well are you?" he replied, rolling his rrs and speaking slowly and kindly as ever.

I was done for driving without due care and attention and fined £5 – my last appearance in court for a traffic offence (so far). But worse than that, I had no car and was to go without for several years.

4

Borrowed Plumes

My student days were over (if student days are ever really over). I was a young minister of religion living in Plympton just east of Plymouth. 'When Plymouth was a fuzzy down, Plympton was a thriving town' and it was still properly independent of Plymouth in my day. I was responsible for four chapels and was part-time chaplain of a large mental hospital.

An old man from one of my congregations fell ill and was dying. His son and his wife had a chip shop in Plymouth. They moved the old man to their flat above the shop so that they could look after him. In those days before the advent of modern drugs, ministers often sat with families to try to ease the path from life to death. In this case, we decided that we would do turn and turn about, alternate nights, so that the young couple could get some sleep. Every other evening I cycled in from Plympton and every other morning I cycled back out again.

The old man had not lived the best of lives and was

finding it difficult facing what he saw as the last judgement.

But his *final* years had been well lived and eventually he was able to die in peace.

It was while he was ill that his son suddenly said to me, "Why don't you borrow our car while this is going on. We've got my dad's car so we don't need ours."

I jumped at the offer, took the keys and went out to where the car was parked, backed close to a wire fence. I switched on the engine – no handle to turn on this black Vauxhall, although it still had a handle just in case. First gear and away – except that Vauxhalls only had three forward gears, as I learned when the car went backwards into the fence!

But I had no further problems.

Christmas was just around the corner. I asked if I could use the car to visit my parents in Reigate in Surrey after I had completed my Christmas Day services. I would travel up on Christmas Day, spend Boxing Day with them and then come back.

They didn't hesitate. So, on Christmas Day, in the afternoon, I set off for Surrey. With Honiton safe behind me I came to that long hill where Aubrey had had such problems. As I put my foot down I smiled at the memory. As the radiator boiled over the smile left my face. In point of fact it boiled over six times on that journey and several times on the way back. When I told the couple, the son said, "Oh yes, I ought to have warned you that you needed to drive it a bit gently."

His father survived for a couple of weeks more and finally died peacefully and without fear.

I returned the car. We held the old man's funeral and

about a week later I cycled into Plymouth to see how the couple were getting on. When I arrived at their chip shop it was all boarded up. Strange. What could possibly have happened. I knocked on a neighbouring door and a lady opened it.

"I've just come to see your neighbours following on from his father's death."

"Well I'm afraid you've had a wasted journey. They did a midnight flit. I don't know any of the details but the police have been round here. They asked a lot of questions I couldn't answer, but I did point out the stolen car they were looking for."

I thanked her for her help and set off back to Plympton. Was that stolen car a black Vauxhall, I wondered, a car that had been driven by a minister of religion for a few weeks, including a trip right across the south of England and back?

5

Richard's Rover

Three or four years passed during which I had got married and moved up to Bamber Bridge, near Preston in Lancashire. My work meant that I was cycling several thousand miles a year. One of my congregations bought me a new bike to replace my sports bike. They felt that it was a far more dignified model, much more suitable for a parson. I'm afraid that I wasn't as grateful as I should have been!

We were expecting our first child and my wife was safely out of the way in hospital. It was time to produce a surprise of my own!

When I was still at school I had been given the job of escorting an 'old' man around the premises, so I livened up our tour with all the old stories about the school: ghost stories like 'The Governor's Grey Mare' and tales of boys dancing naked on the lawns in front of the headmaster's house, and so on. Little did I know that as President of the Old Boys' Association, he knew the stories as well as I did. But he enjoyed himself so much that he invited me to stay with him for a weekend at his home in Leigh on Sea in Essex. During the weekend he taught me Mahjong and he drove me around the area in his lovely Rover – one of those superb, wonderfully comfortable and roomy old Rovers with a facility on the gear shift to enable you to flick into neutral on a long downhill stretch and just glide (illegal now, of course – all the real pleasures in life are made illegal before too long).

I never took to Mahjong (or to any other table or card game come to that) but I did take to the car. One day I would have a Rover of my own – and now it was time for our baby to be born. Why not celebrate? In Preston I found an old Rover 16 – just right. So I bought it and when Richard was born he and his mother went home in style.

Yet that was not what was remembered about that day. Two other things seemed to have much greater significance. The first was that I failed to take any baby clothes to the hospital, so Richard went home in his hospital glad-rags. The second was that I got his birth date wrong in the announcement in the newspaper! What trivialities compared with a drive home in a Rover otherwise known as the 'poor man's Rolls'.

Soon after his birth we took him to see my parents. It was a long and comfortable journey, but with only four of the six cylinders of the engine working, it seemed to find the hills quite a struggle.

When we arrived I told my dad that I needed to arrange for it to be repaired before we went home. We drove to the garage he used. While we were there my dad suggested that we should try out a brand new green Morris 1000. "You drive," he said.

It was beautiful. You could almost drive it with your

little finger, it was so light. Of course, it wasn't to be compared with my old Rover. It was a bit tinny, to tell the truth, but it was certainly nice to drive.

We returned to the garage. "It's yours," said my dad, "provided you trade in your old Rover. On your income (£360 a year) you can't afford to drive that Rover but this will do you very well."

Even though I had never intended to drive my car more than about once a week, he was right, of course. But once again, I wasn't anywhere near as grateful as I should have been.

And I was even less grateful when I found that the heater didn't work – well, not until I had taken it out and put it back in upside down! It served us very well for the next four years in spite of a good deal of misuse. In those days before seat belts there were times when I carried as many as eight scouts or eleven wolf cubs in her. By the time we were off to India the pure air of the industrial north had turned her into something of a rust bucket, but my dad took her back from me and gave her to my brother Aubs. Although he was six years older than me it was his first car and served him very well.

6

The Famous Ford

In 1961 we went to South India, to a small town called Medak, 60 miles north of the twin cities of Secunderabad and Hyderabad. We didn't need a car very often and for most of the time we didn't have one. There were single decker buses from the coach station across the road to the city.

Actually we were woken each morning by the muezzin call from the local mosque and by the coach station radio calling, "Horlicks, drink Horlicks, ba-doom, ba-doom."

For long journeys there were the trains, one of the few decent legacies from the days of the Raj. And locally we got around on the most comfortable bikes I have ever ridden in my life. The saddles were as well cushioned as motorbike seats. I doubt if my boys were quite as comfortable though, with one of them on the back luggage carrier and the other on a small saddle on the crossbar. Andrew, our second son, had been born soon after Richard in Lancashire. But the bikes were ideal for cycling out to local villages through the forest and past the paddy fields where the rice was grown.

If we DID need a car we could often borrow either the bishop's or the hospital's Willys Jeep. But there came a time when fellow missionaries went on leave for six months and they had an old Ford Anglia, so they lent it to us. For a while I found it almost impossible to start. But our garage space was four feet above the drive so, with a gentle push, a run down onto the drive with the car in gear and the clutch ready, it would start every time from home.

I pulled into a garage for petrol and told the Indian lad who filled it that I would need a push to get started.

"Oh no, sir. These will start *every* time. No trouble if you are knowing how."

He explained the knack and he was right. She started every time. No trouble for the rest of her time with us. In fact, the only time we ever had any trouble with her was when we had to go to Bangalore, 500 miles to the south of us. There were the four of us and a doctor, a close friend called Audrey who was going to share the driving with me.

I wrote the story of this journey in my book *In Travellings Often* which has been out of print for a long time – and I no longer have a copy so I'm writing now from memory.

We had looked at a map and talked to people about the journey and we planned to do it in two stages, spending the night with missionaries about half way to Bangalore. The monsoon season was just beginning.

I'm not quite sure how far we had got when we had our first puncture, but changing the wheel was no great problem. Somewhere along the line we must have had it repaired and not long after that the exhaust fell off!

We drove noisily southwards. There came a point in the journey where we had chosen to use a shortcut, turning left off the highway for about fifty miles. We soon learned why most people preferred the longer journey. Our shortcut was little more than an English bridleway. We crawled and bumped our way along until at last we reached a decent road again.

And then, as evening came and darkness, the rain began to fall. The headlights were not too brilliant. The windscreen wipers were not too brilliant either, although they were better than Aubrey's had been. As we entered the town which was our destination for the night, I got out and stood on the running board with the passenger window slightly open so that I could shout instructions to Audrey, who was driving. Suddenly, "STOP!" I yelled, and Audrey did just that.

She was just in time. We were driving straight into the river. She backed out, turned round and we managed to find the place where we were staying.

Our first task the following morning was to cross that river on the bund. In flood it looked as though it was 100 yards from one side to the other and I wasn't at all sure whether to risk trying to get across. But the exhaust had fallen off, which meant that there was a bit more clearance below the car. We sat and watched bullock carts crossing the bund. Eventually I decided to risk it. I reckoned we could just about make it.

Very slowly we moved through the water. Then there was a shout from the two boys in the back, "Dad, there's water coming in. It's all round our feet!"

It was in the boot as well and in our trunk busy staining all of our clothes, but we still managed to make our way forwards until we were through. Phew! And I think that must have been when we had our second puncture. In those days garages were few and far between in India but eventually we came to a small town which boasted a garage. There we rested while (without bothering to remove our trunk from the boot) Indian lads swarmed all over the car, mending the puncture and replacing the exhaust as well as filling the car up with petrol. Eventually we drove off in style with a nice quiet car. And we only had one more puncture before we reached our destination.

Two or three months later, Audrey and I made the return journey, this time sticking to the main highway, even if it was a rather longer journey. Before we started, neither of us had said anything but I think both of us had made the same decision. We were going to do that 500 miles in one day – and we did, without a single mishap. What a remarkable car that famous Ford Anglia had proved to be.

The only other car I drove in India was a Hindustan Ambassador (a Morris Oxford built under licence in India). After the Ford it seemed the height of luxury and when, many years later, a garage in London imported some of them I was sorely tempted. £4,000 for a brand new Ambassador! It seemed a must, but when my mechanic asked me if I really wanted to go back to using a grease gun every thousand miles, I realised that cars had moved on and I resisted the temptation.

7

India

Let's step aside from my life with cars for a moment or two.

When I first learned that we were going to live on the edge of a small town in the heart of the Indian countryside, in the seclusion of a mission compound, two images came to mind. Our mission compound was to prove to be a huge estate enclosing a large school, a hospital, a cathedral, a village and a few scattered houses of which ours was one. The images that came to my mind were both of them wonderfully peaceful: the calm and quiet of a Cathedral Close; and the loveliness of the English countryside.

I was soon to learn that the two words 'India' and 'quiet' do not belong together. I have already mentioned that we were woken each morning, early, by the muezzin call and by the coach station loudspeakers. The noise of the coach station, across the road just a couple of hundred yards away, was with us all day.

But we had plenty of other noises of our own, especially in the evening and at night. In the small reservoirs from which we watered the garden there were frogs. In the trees there were cicadas (crickets). There were also brain-fever birds in the trees with the most monotonous bird 'song' you could ever wish to hear, and it went on and on. And in the wider compound there were donkeys. I have never heard braying like it. I was told that they were all male and that their braying was in desperation for females. True or false? I don't know but they certainly made a racket. And if, late at night, you finally thought you were going to get a bit of peace, a dog might bark – correction, almost certainly would bark. Immediately from all around there would be replies from the jackals that lived in the wild. On and on it would go because the jackals would set ALL the dogs off.

Of course, jackals weren't the only wild things around. There were plenty of monkeys. Fascinating, charming, loveable things? Forget it. They invaded houses and terrorised the people who lived there. But worse than that, they invaded the hospital. One of our Indian doctors applied for a gun licence to kill them but he was turned down because, of course, there is a Hindu monkey god. His second application for a licence to kill pests was also turned down. But when he applied for a gun for self-defence the application was granted, enabling him to shoot monkeys.

Fortunately our little dachsund was a match for monkeys, and for the mongoose which wished to steal our hens' eggs, and for the rats which plagued us. There were two kinds. She caught and killed the ordinary brown rat. But there was another with a poisonous bite. These she caught and tossed up into the air until they were finally so bemused that they could be killed. There was a third rat the size of a cat which we thankfully hardly ever saw.

Our dog Toni was also wonderfully good with cobras. She had a special whine just for them, alerting us to their presence and then keeping them occupied until we arrived with sticks to kill them. There were plenty of other snakes too. I had read somewhere that snakes do not cross concrete, so I knew we were quite safe upstairs, even though we had an outside staircase, because the stairs were made of concrete. One morning I had washed and then my wife followed me. Screams and running feet suggested that something might be wrong. There were three snakes in the bathroom and I hadn't noticed!

Only once did we have a special treat – and it really was special because these animals have now almost completely disappeared in the wild. We were driving home one night and caught a tiger in our headlights. I slowed and stopped. Quietly we watched it for a moment or two before it slipped away from the edge of the road and was lost to view.

I spent a lot of time in the countryside, cycling through the forests or by the rice fields out to small villages. Most of what I saw on these trips was a variation on what you can see here on farmland. There were sheep (tails down) and goats (tails up); there were not many cows but large numbers of water buffalo. Once, cycling along with a friend and chatting, not looking where I was going, I rode straight into the side of a water buffalo. It took no notice at all, but I came off my bike.

I was told that there were bears in the forest but never saw them. Very rarely there would be a glimpse of a deer and there were herds of small wild pigs and tribes of monkeys, but nothing else.

Here in the forest perhaps you would expect to find a bit

of peace and quiet. Not a bit of it. People, especially Lambardis, the local gypsy people, went out into the forest to collect wood. Two of them, a quarter of a mile or so apart, would have a chat. In a special tone of voice they could make themselves heard without any trouble.

So it wasn't until we came home to England that we found places of peace again. They are less and less common. We are retired now and living in Dorset, a county without motorways. And yet, even here, it grows increasingly difficult to find places where there is no background hum of road noise. And that is especially true now that we are growing less and less able to walk off the beaten track.

8

Beryl the Bedford

When we came back to England I spent a few months travelling far and wide telling people about the church in India. I bought a Hillman Minx.

And then the church stationed me in Alfreton in Derbyshire with responsibilities which were to grow, looking after a large number of chapels, most of which had no future.

Alfreton itself was quite a decent town and the countryside to the west of it was wonderful, although very few local people ever seemed to visit it.

East of Alfreton was where most of my work lay, on the borders of Derbyshire and Nottinghamshire. It was coal mining country and the mines were closing down. The men led hard lives down the pits, and having worked on their doorsteps all their lives they weren't about to travel to work when their pits closed. So there was a general air of an area that was dying, an air of hopelessness, grey and miserable.

Most of the chapels were dying. I would imagine that

they are gone now. Their congregations were very small but on Sundays they had to have the services they had always had.

But what about mid-week? Many of them had little tiny groups of people who met mid-week for a 'talk' by a visiting speaker (often me) and more importantly, a cup of tea and a chat. But just suppose. . .

And so it was that the Hillman Minx was replaced by Beryl the Bedford Minibus.

Behind the driver's seat she had a bench seat running crosswise and behind that there were two more bench seats along the sides of the van – room for the driver and ten people all sitting in a measure of discomfort and without seat-belts to help them keep their seats.

But it was now possible to pick up a group of ladies from one village and give them a little trip to another village, and then hold a meeting with twice as many people.

But Beryl had other uses because our family was growing. There were now two daughters: Jean and Christine. When we drove south to see our parents, the pram fitted perfectly between the two back bench seats with my younger daughter in it. The two boys stretched out on the two bench seats either side of the pram and my elder daughter stretched out on the bench behind us, with my wife and I in the front. But although we always travelled overnight my elder daughter never seemed to go to sleep. She was the one who chatted to her dad and enabled him to keep awake on the long night journeys.

However, Beryl was primarily a working vehicle. And just as she was useful for carrying groups of women about, so she was also useful for taking isolated youngsters to places where there were other youngsters – thus making them feel that they weren't the only teenagers still going to chapel. And of course, when it was party time for my own children – birthdays for example – I could fill the van with their pals, take them out into the countryside and dump them while I had a quiet read. And when they came back from their adventures I could stuff them with unsuitable and unhealthy food like crisps, pop and so on. All very irresponsible and non-PC.

While we were living in Alfreton one of my brothers-in-law came to live with us, and in one of the villages to the east of us he found a lovely girl. For him she was irresistible. So Beryl began to come into her own as a courting vehicle too. One night Pete came home distressed and fuming. How could he tell me what had happened? Beryl had been parked outside his girlfriend's house, as large as life and clearly visible:

"Bliddy drunken Pole drove right into the back of 'er."

The damage wasn't THAT bad, but I took her to be repaired. When I got to the garage there were the usual oohs and aahs and then the foreman said, "Instead of having her repaired, why don't you trade her in as she is and replace her with something new?"

I'd never thought of that, but our time in Derbyshire was drawing to a close and my next job wouldn't need a minibus, so I came away the proud owner of Rosie the Renault 4.

With a bench seat in front and a bench seat behind there was room for the six of us and a surprising amount of room for luggage in the boot. All right, so she was a bit tinny but she was comfortable, warm, economical and thoroughly reliable. She was a superb little car and her rather odd gear stick gave her just that extra hint of character.

44

However, she did have one fault, as I was to learn one night. Because it was night-time I had decided to drive right through London instead of around it. Back in the 1960s (swinging though they might have been), London in the early hours was pretty quiet. As I drove into North London my clutch cable snapped, leaving me in top gear. It proved to be a remarkable top gear. By slowing almost to stalling point and accelerating hard in other places, and watching as far ahead as I possibly could, I managed to use or mis-use the traffic lights and go right through London from north to south without stopping once, and so arrived safely at my destination.

When we came to replace the cable we found that it ran over a metal right-angle which inevitably slowly frayed the cable until it snapped. A spare cable became an essential piece of equipment.

However, with four children it was becoming clear that there was no way we would ever be able to afford to go on holiday – unless perhaps we took our own home with us! But there was no way that Rosie would be able to tow a caravan big enough for all of us.

So Rosie was traded in for an older Vauxhall Victor, again with bench seats and with the gear stick on the steering column. Vera became one of my all time favourite cars. She was a real pleasure to drive and wonderfully comfortable. Before long she was joined by Charlie the Caravan, a very solid, rather heavy, Pemberton Diamond. These two had some wonderful adventures together. I told their story in my book *Happy Endings* and I think it bears repeating here.

But there was one little tale I didn't tell. My boys and I had been down to Wiltshire – to Salisbury – and we were on the way home. We made a loo stop in a large, more or less empty, gravel car park. I took longer than the boys and when I came out they were looking a bit – well, sort of, uncomfortable. Perhaps abashed is the right word.

They had been throwing stones and one of them had broken the rear screen. Because it was the rear screen I think they suffered more than I did.

Twice in my driving life I've had front windscreens go and that is a great deal more unpleasant.

9

Vera and Charlie

I don't know why it is, but sometimes people don't believe the stories I tell. But if anyone doubts this one, all they have to do is to ask my children. They will tell you that every word of it is true – more or less.

It was quite a long time after we lived in India – long enough to have added two girls to the family – that we began caravanning. We bought a sturdy (and heavy) four berth Pemberton Diamond caravan called Charlie and we put in two extra bunks for the girls. In spite of her brand new tow bar, the only person who was not excited by our new purchase was Vera, our special Vauxhall Victor with a bench front seat.

She felt that she was too old to be introduced to new adventures and that it was beneath her dignity to be used to tow a caravan. And when she met Charlie for the first time she was decidedly frosty even if she did manage to be very polite. I introduced them shortly before bringing Charlie home.

"Vera, this is Charlie. Charlie, this is Vera."

"Mornin' missus," said Charlie. "Pleased ter meet yer."

"Good morning, Charles," replied Vera. "I trust that we shall travel the road smoothly together."

"Cor blimey," whispered Charlie to me. "She's a bit toffee-nosed int she?"

"Yes she is," I said. "But it's only her way. She's a very nice car really. Don't take any notice of her posh talk and you'll get on well."

"Stop whispering, you two," interrupted Vera. "Don't you know that it is very rude to whisper in company?"

"Sorry ma'am," said Charlie. "I was just tellin' the guvnor what an honour it will be to be towed by a proper lady such as yerself."

"Oh," exclaimed Vera, and she sounded very pleased. "Well Charles, I'm sure that we shall get on very well as long as you remember that I am the leader."

Charlie grinned and winked at me, whispering even more quietly, "I don't think I shall forget that, do you?"

I hitched the two up and Vera towed Charlie home. She was none too happy. After all, Charlie was pretty heavy. But she perked up when I said:

"Well done, Vera. You've brought Charlie home just in time because we are all going on holiday to the Isle of Wight."

"A holiday," she said. "That will be most acceptable. Let us hope that the weather will be propitious and that the sun will shine brightly."

"You do realise that Charlie will be coming, too?"

"Oh," exclaimed Vera. "Oh no, I don't think that will do at all. No. Positively not."

"Why not?" I asked. "We'll tow him to some lovely

48

Leslie on his first motorbike.

Aubrey the Austin 7
1934 vintage

The Ford Anglia (A54A) from Leslie's time in India.

Leslie and Wendy's
first house purchase.

An inside picture from
that first house.

Leslie's wife Wendy.

Two chauffeur hire
Alpha Cars
outside Leslie's
bungalow.
Jaguar *(left)*
Daimler *(right)*

Two more
Alpha Cars
from Leslie's
chauffeur car
hire business.

The red Ford minibus.
Part of the Alpha Cars stable.

One of the Alpha Cars attending a wedding:
a white Jaguar 4.2 litre.

spot, perhaps in green fields by a river or somewhere overlooking the sea. It will be idyllic."

"It may sound idyllic to you," Vera replied sourly. "But think of all the luggage you take when you go on holiday, and who is it who has to carry the luggage? Now, on top of all that you speak of towing Charlie but it is not 'we' who will tow him. It is 'I' and that is too much to ask of an elderly lady such as myself."

"Oh, come on, Vera," I said. "You aren't elderly," (although quietly I had to admit that she wasn't as young as she once was) you're still young, strong and healthy and you've got a beautiful new tow bar. Besides, just think of all your horse power. Why, one horse could pull Charlie so you will pull him easily."

"Please do not insult me by associating me with horses – nasty big, smelly things that make a mess on the roads."

"Oh, very well," I laughed. "But I still say that you are quite strong enough to tow Charlie, especially as we shall give him all the luggage to carry."

"And if he carries the luggage that just gives me extra weight to tow. And you are forgetting, are you not (why can't she just say 'aren't you' like anybody else?), that in addition to towing Charlie fully laden with heavy holiday luggage, I shall also be expected to carry six persons and no doubt your wife will find my empty boot too much of a temptation. She will fill that as well."

"Well yes, I see what you mean. . . but the children aren't very heavy," I said cheerfully. "Nor, come to that, is my wife."

"Be that as it may," answered Vera. "The load will be too great. My springs will never stand the strain. If you are

49

going to overload me in this unkind and unnatural fashion, my springs will need a special attachment to make them stronger."

"Stuff and nonsense," I exclaimed crossly. "Why you have only just been overhauled and serviced."

"And very pleasant it was too. That nice young man in the garage handles me beautifully. Nevertheless, I warn you. Although it is true that I do retain something of my youthful charm and beauty, I am no longer as young as I once was.

"Indeed, you have given me a great deal of work to do in my time, so my springs are not as springy as they were in the spring of my life."

"Relax," I said. "You'll be fine. I'll drive you very gently, so don't you worry about your springs."

So we loaded up Charlie, and I'm sorry to say that Vera was right. With all that lovely space available, my wife couldn't resist filling up the boot as well. After all, you never know what you might want. At last everything was ready and we set off.

"Now Vera," I repeated. "I'm going to drive you very gently because you have such a heavy load. So don't you worry about your springs."

But Vera did worry. Every time she was taken over a hole in the road or a big bump, her springs groaned. Even though I drove so carefully, there were still times when she thought her springs would break, but they didn't.

We drove for a long time before reaching the New Forest. In those days, you could park or camp where you liked in the forest. We stopped in a small glade and I took the children into the forest to let off steam while the missus got busy in the caravan and made some lunch.

We sat around the caravan tables and stuffed on

beautiful big home-made beef burgers and drank coke or coffee – good, healthy food!

We cleared up carefully, making sure that we didn't leave any litter anywhere, and then set off for Lymington. It didn't take all that long to get there.

"Who's going to be the first to see the sea?" I asked.

They all saw it at the same time and shouted, "I saw it. I saw it first."

"No you didn't."

"I did."

"You didn't."

"Oh, be quiet all of you. I can't hear myself think."

We drove quietly down to the dock and the car ferry was already waiting for us. We were the very first to park. Soon there were lots of cars and vans behind us and beside us. Lots and lots and lots of them.

Because we were first, we were the very first to go onto the ferry. A large ramp joined the boat to the dock. We drove gently down the slope to the ramp and then a bit more powerfully up onto the ramp. As Vera began to go upwards, Charlie was still coming down. All his weight was thrown onto the back of the car.

"Ooh," groaned the springs. "Ooh, OOH," and then with a loud noise they went snap.

By this time Charlie was coming up again and so we drove to the other end of the ferry where we would be the first to get off.

"What was that awful noise?" asked my wife.

"It was right underneath us," chorused three voices from the back.

"It sounds as though Vera was right," I said, and I was feeling very worried.

"Of course I was right," snapped Vera. "I am always right. You have broken my springs."

"I'm sorry, but perhaps if we are very careful we can get to the campsite and then I can take you to a garage and have you seen to. Now you just have a nice rest while we all go and have a look around the ferry."

The ferry set off from Lymington and began to cross the sea to the Isle of Wight. We explored the ferry and bought ourselves some drinks. We watched the land behind us as we drew further and further away and then we watched the island as we drew closer and closer.

Then the captain told us all to return to our cars and get ready to land. So we went back to Vera and Charlie and waited.

After a little while the ferry came to a halt. There was a loud noise as the ramp in front of Vera began to drop slowly down until it lay on the ground. Then one of the sailors waved to us to drive off. I drove slowly forward down the ramp and then up onto the island.

At least, that is what I tried to do. Everything went smoothly while Vera was going down, out of the ship. But when she tried to climb up onto land, Charlie's weight pressed down on her. With no springs, the car came down firmly onto the wheels and stopped them moving. They were stuck fast. They couldn't move and that meant that no one else could move either.

The sailors waved to me to tell me to get a move on. The cars behind Charlie began to rev their engines angrily. I grew red in the face and pleaded with Vera.

"Come on, come on."

But Vera couldn't come on. She couldn't budge. The cars behind began to toot their horns. Drivers leaned out of their windows and shouted at us. The sailors waved us forward angrily.

Charlie said, "Oh my gawd, oh my gawd," over and over again.

Vera was the only one who was not in a flap. She looked about her and said, "I fear that we are most seriously incommoded. There is only one thing for it. You will have to unhitch me from Charles and then you will have to get some nice strong men to lift my rear bumper while I am driven slowly off the ferry."

"But what about me?" shouted Charlie.

"Ah," sighed Vera happily. "That is not my problem. I can do nothing about you."

The hooting and tooting and shouting grew louder and louder. I ran to the sailors and told them what had happened. They ran to the drivers of the other cars. Soon men were jumping out all over the place and swarming all around us. They unhitched Charlie.

They lifted Vera's rear bumper and the whole back of the car until the wheels were free, and then they ran behind Vera while I drove carefully forward and into a lay-by at the side of the road.

"Wonderful," exclaimed Vera. "All those big strong handsome men and all for me."

But I'm afraid I wasn't listening. I ran back to Charlie and with all the other men helping, pulled him off the ferry and up to the lay-by behind Vera. I have never had so much help in all my life. Now, at last, all the other cars and vans and lorries could get off the ferry. They waved and tooted and cheered happily this time, and away they went.

My wife and children had kept very quiet all this time because they didn't want me to lose my temper. I went off

53

to phone the AA to get Vera to a garage where she could be repaired. The others got into Charlie and had some tea. Then they played games until at last I came back with Vera.

She had new springs with added strengtheners and she was feeling fine, especially as she had been the centre of attention. And of course, she kept on reminding me that she had been right all along and I should have listened to her. Oh yes! She was feeling fine, but I can't say that I was.

We hitched up to Charlie and Vera said, "Come Charles. All is now well and we shall make good progress to our nocturnal resting place."

"Wot the 'eck is she on about?" asked Charlie quietly.

"She means that it won't be long before we get to the campsite," I told him. But it was plenty long enough. The site was right at the southern tip of the island, half a mile from the lighthouse, and it was dark when we finally arrived.

I didn't take too much notice of the precise spot where we stopped. We just unhitched Charlie, put his legs down, got our beds ready, had some supper and went to bed. We were all fast asleep in no time.

"Good night, Charles," whispered Vera. "We have had a small measure of excitement today have we not?"

"Yeah," answered Charlie. "You're darned right we 'ave," and he and Vera also went to sleep.

And that should have been that, but it wasn't. In the middle of the night, I became aware that one of the girls was crying. Now I'm not very good at the best of times but I am very far from being at my best in the middle of the night when it is pitch black, with not even a street light to guide me.

I struggled out of bed and whispered, "It's all right. I'm coming." But was I? I couldn't see a thing. Luckily the caravan was not very big. I felt my way down the van until I reached the children's bed and bunk bed. And all the time one of the girls was crying.

"It's all right. I'm here," I felt around on the top bunk and found Christine. She was all right. I felt around for Jean. Where had she got to? I couldn't find her. At last the truth dawned on me. She wasn't there! She'd rolled over and rolled right out of the window!

Now, at last, I did begin to hurry. Out I went in my bare feet, and through the long grass around the caravan to the other side. And there I found Jean lying in her sleeping bag in the long grass. How lucky it was that the grass was long and how lucky that it was dry. Jean was completely unhurt.

I picked her up and carried her back into the van. I closed and fastened the window and moved Christine over to be beside the window. Then I lifted Jean onto the bunk.

"There. You'll be perfectly safe that side." I kissed her goodnight and went back to bed and was soon fast asleep.

Sometime later on I found I was having a dream. One of the girls was crying. She went on crying. At last it dawned on me that one of the girls WAS crying. Now I'm not very good at the best of times but I am very far from being at my best in the middle of the night when it is pitch black, with not even a street light to guide me.

I struggled out of bed and whispered, "It's all right, I'm coming." But was I? I couldn't see a thing. Luckily the caravan was not very big. I felt my way down the van until I reached the children's bed and bunk bed. And all the time one of the girls was crying.

"It's all right. I'm here," I felt around on the top bunk

55

and found Jean. She was all right. I felt around for Christine. Where had she got to? I couldn't find her. At last the truth dawned on me. She wasn't there!

But she couldn't have gone out of the window. I fastened it myself. . . didn't I?

"Who opened the window?" I growled.

"I did," said Richard. "It's too hot down here."

Now, at last, I began to hurry. Out I went in my bare feet, and through the long grass around the caravan to the other side.

And there I found Christine lying in her sleeping bag in the long grass. How lucky it was that the grass was long and how lucky that it was dry. Christine was completely unhurt.

I picked her up and carried her back into the van. I took her to our double bed at the other end of the van and put her between my wife and myself.

"There, you will be perfectly safe now." I kissed her goodnight and crawled into bed myself and – well no. This time I wasn't soon fast asleep. Have you ever tried sleeping right on the edge so that you won't disturb the others?

10

From Perky to a Daimler

1973 was to prove to be an awful year with an awfulness of my own making – yet it began so well. The two boys were in America on a youth exchange. We had two American girls while they were away. And then I was given the chance of a six-week exchange with an American minister.

Sadly I was persuaded that Vera had to go. The American minister would need something 'better'. So I bought a more modern Vauxhall Victor which I didn't like as much as Vera but, as a car, it was perfectly good.

While we were in the USA our marriage fell apart. We also broke a milk jug and did our level best to replace it but couldn't find like for like. Eventually I bought a new one and left 60 dollars for them to replace it with something more satisfactory. And I drove their Ford and marvelled at the cheapness of petrol and of many other things too. My English stipend was just adequate in England. In India it had raised us to the level of almost rich. In America, although it would buy us far more than in England, it placed us within what they thought of as their poverty levels!

When I returned to England I found that my new Victor was badly dented and scratched, yet there was no word of apology. I left home and went to live with my parents for a while near Worthing. I also left the ministry of the church but continued to go to church. It took quite a while for me to realise that I no longer believed the things I had been preaching and teaching for so long. Well before that day came, I had discovered that a training in theology doesn't really fit you for life in the working world.

Over the next few years I was to do a variety of jobs: typing address labels; debt collecting; selling insurance (I was hopeless at that); producing audio text books for a blind student; and for four years, working in the NHS. But to begin with, I drove taxis – Victors like my own. But my own Victor had been bought with borrowed money so I sold it, repaid the money and bought a pretty old VW Beetle called Perky.

She might have been pretty old but she lived up to her name, Perky, and became a great favourite with my two daughters. She proved to be a sturdy little beggar and although she did a fair mileage in the three years we were together, she only broke down twice (once when I had lent her to someone else!). Sadly, the time came when I could no longer afford to keep her.

It was while I was working in the Health Service that I first met Wendy who became my second wife. The time came when we needed a home, so we started to look for a house. After all, how could I ask Wendy to share my life if I didn't have a home to share with her. Eventually we found somewhere. But we only had £6 between us!

My Dad lent us the deposit. My income enabled us to obtain a mortgage for three thousand pounds but we were still three thousand pounds short. I had to tell the owner that I couldn't raise the money. Fortunately she was so desperate to sell that she lent me what I needed.

I left the Health Service and for a time, failed to earn an adequate income, and then I started working as a part-time driver for a private hire company called Gold Star.

What Wendy endured in those early days was incredible, worth a book in itself. I suppose that most people would say that being married to me guarantees that she has always had to endure a great deal. But in those early days she often walked seven miles to work in the morning and seven miles back again in the evening. Gold Star was to begin to change all that.

I hadn't been with Gold Star long before the owner decided to advertise for a manager. I applied and got the job, a job which entitled me to the use of one of their vehicles. So sometimes Wendy still walked, but sometimes she went to work in a Mercedes or in an older Volvo, or even in the height of luxury, in a clapped out old minibus.

The work was pretty demanding but I did also have a paid holiday.

We were looking forward to going on holiday to Seaton in East Devon with one of the Mercedes. At the last moment the owner told me that I couldn't have a Merc, I would have to take a minibus. I was furious, but it actually gave us a far better holiday. For one thing, sitting up high in a minibus you can see a great deal more than you can in a car. And we took a small Calor gas stove, a kettle and so on, so we were able to make ourselves cups of tea and coffee and small snacks. It was so useful that it was to be the precursor of – well, let me tell you all in good time.

There was one car Gold Star had which I had never seen, an old white Daimler which was hired out for weddings. I first saw the car when the boss was away on holiday. One of the drivers was driving it on the day, so I took him to fetch it from its lock-up garage. All went well until it broke down. The driver called me and we pushed it into a side road to wait for the owner's return. Unfortunately the side road was part of a private estate and people grumbled to the police. They rang me and told me to move it, so I did. And it was then that I noticed things which the police hadn't noticed.

The car was not taxed. Nor was it insured. When the owner returned I blew my top and in my time with the firm the car was never booked out again. But my time was coming to an end. I had decided to take the risk of trying to establish my own firm, which meant buying a car, and not any old car. Living where we were in Surrey, I wanted to try tapping the top of the market, so I had to have a good car. Mercedes was everyone's favourite because they were so reliable and went on for ever. But I had driven a Jaguar for one of our customers and preferred it – and it had the advantage of being British.

I hadn't made up my mind either way but I began looking out for one or the other.

One day I was at a garage in Walton on Thames and saw a brown Daimler sitting there. I had a good look around it. It seemed to be in excellent condition. I tried the driver's door and it was open so I got in and had a look around. It was immaculate and an automatic. If you were doing a lot of driving in London you needed an automatic. I'd driven up there a fair bit with a gear-box Merc and it was murder.

A man came across and I got out of the car.

"Like it, do you?"

"It looks very nice and seems to have been kept by somebody who really cared for it. How much is it going for?"

The man laughed. "It's not for sale. It's my car and has just been serviced."

I felt embarrassed. "I'm so sorry. I thought this was one of the cars for sale on the forecourt."

"You really like it, do you?"

"Yes, very much. I'm so sorry."

He paused and then he said, "Actually, it will be for sale in a few weeks if you're really interested. I'm being promoted and there's a car that goes with my new job. I don't really want to sell but there will be no sense in hanging on to this."

We talked some more – we talked money – and there, weeks later, I became the proud owner of a brown Daimler. Alpha Cars was born.

While I was with Gold Star I learned one important lesson that was to help sustain me throughout my driving career. I learned to make the most of my times alone in the car. I carefully worked on obtaining a reputation as the slowest driver we had. If I went to Heathrow or Gatwick with a customer I always stopped on the way back for a walk by the Thames or in the Surrey countryside. Of course, they still had to be fairly short walks, but when I became my own boss the walks became longer and helped make the job really pleasurable.

A lot of work with celebrities involved very unsocial

hours. But when the weary night's work was finally over I would dawdle home and often see foxes. And it was on one of those dawdles that I saw my first badger and watched him for a while. On the very worst of those long nights (apart from driving all-night party-goers) I would find myself driving home between 4 and 5 in the morning (before leaving home again at 7). I would pull into a lay-by or pull up on a quieter lane and listen to the dawn chorus. There are very few experiences more wonderful than that, especially when you are feeling a bit sour because people can be incredibly inconsiderate at times. These were moments of cleansing, purifying and refreshing – sheer magic.

11

Alpha Cars

You have to be a bit mad to buy a house when you have no money. You also have to be a bit mad to decide to start up your own business when you have no money.

I worked out what I would need, doubled it and went to see my bank manager. He said if I could show that I had half what I needed he would lend me the rest. So I went round my family and friends and borrowed what I needed 'for three months'. The bank lent me the other half and three months later, having repaid the loans, there was nothing left in my account, but by then I had my Daimler and I was up and running.

My two years with Gold Star helped in a number of ways. First, I had learned the nature of the business. Second, I had got to know the other firms in the area and had a good relationship with them all, so I could sub-contract work I couldn't do myself. But I also knew that they would sub-contract work to me, and in the early days that was a wonderful help.

Third, and perhaps most important of all, I had got to

know Bob, a first-rate mechanic, who was to look after all my vehicles down through the years.

And last but not least, Gold Star customers knew my telephone number from weekends when I had been on duty. I tried to be honourable. Time after time they would ring me and I would explain that I was no longer with Gold Star, but I would pass on their booking. But after a while, one or two people rang and said:

"No, don't pass on the booking. I want you."

Meanwhile I had walked miles delivering a classy leaflet advertising my services and that produced one or two customers who were to be with me for the next twenty years.

Right from the beginning it was clear that I was going to need someone to look after the telephone when I was driving and, at the second attempt, I was very lucky. George, a housebound, disabled chap applied for the job and looked after things for many years. He had been knocked down on the 1st January 1939 and lost a leg. He always said that he was lucky because it saved him going to war.

Nor was it long before I needed a second car, but there was the usual problem – I had no money. It was one of my customers who was pushing me, so I told him that, though I agreed with him, I hadn't got the money to buy. So he lent me the money as long as I guaranteed that he would always have one of our own cars and never be sub-contracted to anyone else. For a long time, every month I would send him my bill and he would pay nothing, but eventually we were all square.

He was one of the most difficult customers I ever had, always trying to knock my prices down and very demanding, treating both my driver and me (when I was driving) as lackeys. Once in the car he would sit in the back with a stack of files and begin dictating into a machine. When the journey to London was over, we would be sent back with what he had dictated so that his secretary could get on with it.

Once, when I was driving with him out of London on the A3, he was in the back, as usual, with a pile of papers and files. We topped the brow of a hill and I slammed on the brakes to avoid smashing into a tailback of vehicles in every lane. For a while the air was blue and I was named with all the foul names under the sun. This would certainly be the last time he ever used me, and so on.

And then he fell quiet. When we arrived he got out of the car and apologised, thanking me for avoiding a smash. In the end he was to prove immensely helpful to me, not just over the second car, but in a variety of ways. He was at his most valuable when we wanted to move house. We had found a bungalow that we wanted, but when we looked into it we needed my income to be three times what it was in order to get a mortgage. I talked to him about it. He was a solicitor. He asked, if he could help me to get the bungalow, would I let him handle the deal?

Of course I would. So he told me how to set about it. I went home and took my accounts for the last three years and re-wrote them in such a way as to show that my income was three times what it actually was. Then he sent me to an accountant who was prepared to write a letter confirming that these accounts were a true record. That letter was pretty expensive, but the combination of his letter and my accounts enabled me to get the mortgage I needed and we got the bungalow we wanted. In another three years my income had risen to the required level! If you are foolish enough or wicked enough there is a way round most problems.

My second car was a Jaguar 4.2. These two were to be the first of seventeen Daimlers and Jaguars over the years – never more than three at a time. They were the backbone of our work and for a number of years, the only cars we ran – and, of course, each additional car meant that we needed an additional driver. One of the first, Roy, was to prove to be one of the best, if not the very best that I ever had.

One of my nieces used to ask me, "Have you driven anybody famous recently, Uncle Leslie?"

As it happens, we drove quite a lot of famous people. Some of them we drove just for one-off journeys and some of them we drove regularly for years. There were opera singers and dancers; pop stars; stars of stage, screen, radio and sport. One of the actors was brilliant with accents and had a vivid imagination. I remember one journey from Euston to his home in Surrey where he had me in tears the whole journey and struggling to see to drive. Needless to say, the tears were tears of merriment.

There were also a few diplomats of different countries. And politicians, including a couple of cabinet ministers. But I've decided not to name any of them. Why? Supremely because celebrities are no more significant to me than anybody else.

Think about it for a moment. How did they get to be celebrities? Some of them were born to it – their celebrity was an accident of birth or marriage. Others were men and women of one marketable talent, a talent which had been blown up and exploited with considerable success. So they were often in the public eye, and there were amusing moments when I was able to help them preserve a measure of privacy, avoiding the press or avoiding fans; and I've experienced the doubtful pleasure of driving with a police escort for a little way.

But none of that makes these people any more significant than any other and oddly enough, they were often not very interesting to drive. Take some of them outside their own sphere of excellence and they were, I was going to say nothing but that is perhaps a little too unkind. But they were certainly no more knowledgeable or interesting than anybody else. And of course, some of them travelled as if there was no driver in the car at all!

Oddly enough, this business of celebrity was to raise its head in the other work I was doing, work which came to take over my life. I'll tell the story elsewhere but I became one of the first Humanist Celebrants, mainly conducting funerals. As the years went by and the British Humanist Association woke up to the potential of our work, some leading humanists also began to be obsessed with celebrities and wanted to know whenever any of us took the funeral of such people. I never told them, but of course there have been some. To me the most amusing moment was when I, as an ex-Able Seaman Writer, took the funeral of an Admiral!

I wonder how many thousand life stories I have told in my lifetime? Often the most interesting and fascinating life stories are those of people who seemed to the world to be completely insignificant. And certainly, the most valuable people in the world are often those quiet, reliable, unnoticed people who get on with their lives without fuss and without making waves.

So I'm not going to name names. As a businessman, of course, the acid test was how swiftly people paid their bills, and there was one celebrity I refused to drive because, although he paid up in the end, he took an awful long time about it and wouldn't stick to our time frame. Poor men can't wait for their money – certainly my drivers couldn't wait for theirs.

I've been getting on my high horse in this chapter and I'm going to get onto it again in a minute, and then we can forget high horses and concentrate, as we should, on horsepower!

Although driving celebrities helped build up my business, the backbone of the work came, not from these, but from middle to high ranking businessmen working for some of the best known British and International firms. Their work was regular, dependable, and often interesting. And their hours were marginally less unsociable than the hours kept by some of the stars.

I had to work *all* hours, of course. There was one occasion when one of my best customers arrived at Gatwick and I wasn't standing waiting for him. He found me curled up fast asleep in a chair! There was another occasion when an advertising whizz-kid arrived at Gatwick and told me how exhausted he was.

"Why don't you curl up on the back seat and have a sleep sir. I'll drive very gently."

"I never sleep in a car," he replied – but he took off his shoes and was away in moments.

I drove gently and he slept soundly, which is just as well. It was as I was slowing down outside my own home that it suddenly dawned on me that I had a body in the back to be delivered to his home. I pulled away quietly and he was none the wiser.

On another occasion I drove the same man, and two others in the advertising world, from London to Gatwick. They chattered away the whole time, but there was so much jargon that I hadn't the faintest idea what they were talking about.

Then I drove from Gatwick to Heathrow and picked up three Japanese men and took them into London. They also chattered the whole time – in Japanese – but half the time I DID know what they were talking about because of the odd English word such as 'the River Thames'; 'the Houses of Parliament'; 'Westminster'; 'St. Pauls'; 'the Tower of London'.

Sadly, a few of the businessmen gave themselves quite an addition to their incomes by fiddling their expenses. To a degree I was complicit in this because I knew what was going on but couldn't afford to turn down their business.

Yet, together with corrupt politicians, they would have been the first to condemn some of my drivers. None of my drivers had contracts and most of them were part-timers just doing a school run and other bits and bobs of work. Many of them would have been on benefits of one kind or another, unable to get full-time work, glad of the peanuts I paid them (a little bit over the minimum wage). Although I kept a proper record of what they were paid, they will not have declared their earnings. Scandalous? Immoral?

Although I've never been on benefits, I have known what it is to scrape the bottom of the barrel, so I never begrudged them a penny of what they could add to what the state, in its meanness, gave them.

And unlike those businessmen who would have condemned them so roundly, they were incredibly trustworthy. They kept my vehicles at home and looked after them with a minimum of supervision. Imagine the scope for abusing my trust but (with one exception) they never did. Oh, they would take the wife shopping, and use my trust in little ways like that, but they never abused my trust.

I hate it when wealthy people begrudge the poor whatever pennies they can scrape together from whatever source.

So this time I knew what was going on and was complicit in their misdemeanours and it didn't trouble my conscience at all!

Fortunately I liked most of my customers, both the honest ones and the corrupt ones. And it didn't seem to matter what part of the world they came from. But there was one family of Arab diplomats that I didn't like at all. They would arrive by private jet and we would be driven in convoy through Heathrow to pick them up from the plane itself. There was one occasion when I got cut off from the lead car in the convoy and didn't know where to go, but when I found myself heading for one of the runways I knew that I had gone wrong! Often they would arrive separately: men and adult boys on one plane and women and children on another. The diplomat himself always made an issue of paying his bill (without actually saying anything). I had to wait in the hall of their home until I was called. When I WAS summoned I would have to wait in the presence before finally being given my cheque. No words were spoken.

We took the women shopping and that was quite a nightmare, and we took the teenage boys gadding about in London. They loved to tell me that the British Empire was finished. The world would soon be conquered by the Arab world. They were going to show us who was boss. At that point I would say quietly:

"That is never going to happen."

"Why? Why? What do you mean?"

"First," I would say, "you will have to learn to agree amongst yourselves."

During those 'conversations' I never dreamed that Britain would be fool enough to go to war in the Middle East. Nor did I imagine that the Middle East would descend so tragically into the anarchy and slaughter of the present. I wonder what those boys – middle-aged now – make of it all?

In the end I got so sick of them all that I refused their business. Yet there were other Arabs who were a delight to drive.

Before I leave this chapter behind let me mention two more things. I have already referred to the fact that passengers often chat to one another as if the driver is not there. Drivers have to learn discretion. They hear things they shouldn't hear and they see things they shouldn't see. They also learn things they should know nothing about. Their clients must imagine that they are blind and deaf to everything except the road. For their passengers' well-being drivers' discretion and silence must be absolute.

The second is the question of morality. First of all there was my own dishonesty, misrepresenting my 'wealth' so that I could achieve my goals – the establishment of a business when I had no funds and the purchase of a bungalow when I had inadequate funds or income.

These things never troubled me. Both Wendy and I worked very hard. As a result I always paid my debts and paid them on time. I felt that we deserved everything we achieved. My own morality or ideal is very simple: Never knowingly hurt or harm anybody else and do all the good you can. Sadly, I haven't always managed to live up to even that modest aim.

But I *was* troubled about the fact that I was complicit in the dishonesty of others who misused their expense accounts. In effect, they were stealing from their employers, and because I knew what was going on, I was an accessory. I could have alerted their employers but I suspect that they behaved in just the same way. I could have refused their business at a time when we were finding it desperately hard to make ends meet. But they were among my best customers and by recommending me to others, they often brought me new accounts.

Yet I am still uncomfortable about the fact that I didn't refuse them. If I had done, I'm sure that we would have survived somehow without them. People say that confession is good for the soul. I'm not sure that that is necessarily true – but there is my confession. Make of it what you will.

12

Perks

Drivers are often given tips. On the whole, owners are not. I once knew an owner who used his first name when he was acting as the boss of the firm and his second name when he was driving!

One of the very wealthiest people I ever drove sometimes gave me £2, although he usually let one of his minions actually give it to me. It was £2 in 1976 and it was still £2 in 1996! Mostly tips were given just because it is the thing to do – just as we tip waiters, chambermaids and so on – anyone who provides us with a service and is on poor pay! It is one of those odd relics of wealth and class and privilege which sometimes means that we end up tipping people who are better off than we are. Sadly, very occasionally, tips are used as a means of making sure that the 'servant' knows his or her place! I'm afraid that that tells us more about the donor than the 'servant'.

But from time to time I had a very pleasant surprise, and very occasionally it was a surprise in which Wendy shared. We were once invited to a meal where we sat and were

d

able to chat on familiar terms with one or two sports stars, and on another occasion one of my favourite customers invited us both to her home to share in a family meal.

The first time I ever went to a Happy Eater I was taken there by a German businessman. He was also the first person to take me to the famous Simpson's-in-the-Strand! I took mischievous delight when the waiter refused his *American* Express Card with a snooty:

"We do not accept THOSE here, sir."

I've only been to the Savoy three times in my life. The first time was as a guest of one of my customers for tea. The waiter came and tea was ordered.

"What kind of tea would you like, madam: saloon tea, Earl Grey or China?"

We didn't want either Earl Grey or China tea so we ordered 'saloon' tea, but what on earth was it? My hostess knew the pianist so she sent me over to enquire. For a moment or two he was as baffled as we were, and then it clicked. 'Saloon' tea was Ceylon tea – apparently the change of name to Sri Lanka hadn't made its way to the Savoy.

The second time I went to the Savoy was with a pop star but we didn't get past the door. He was wearing jeans! I once took another pop star to a restaurant in London where he was turned away because he wasn't wearing a tie. I offered him my tie just as I had offered the other one my trousers, but neither took up the offer. These incidents brought back a memory of my own. We were sailing to India on the SS *Canton* in 1961 and I was turned away from the dining deck because I wasn't wearing a jacket.

I haven't mentioned the third occasion I went to the Savoy. My first two visits led me to take my wife and her mother there for tea. Even though it was my treat my mother-in-law insisted on paying for herself. When I told her that her tea cost £5 she never questioned it. Goodness knows what she would have thought if she had known the real price.

Drivers will know the Savoy for one more peculiarity. Is it the only place in this country where the approach and exit road requires drivers to drive on the right-hand side of the road?

There are perhaps three other special treats that came my way that are worth mentioning. Two of them involved football. I had been booked to take some people to Selhurst Park to watch Crystal Palace play Arsenal. Although some of my family had become Arsenal supporters I remained loyal to Crystal Palace, the team of my childhood. I parked the car, dropped my passengers off, and followed them at a distance. A policeman was on point duty, directing the traffic.

"I suppose there's not a hope in hell of getting in to watch the match is there?"

"No sir, no chance at all." He paused and fished in his pocket. "Not unless you'd like to use this ticket, sir. Someone got called away. . ."

I was over the moon and found myself just where we had always gone as kids, near the halfway line. To make matters even better, Palace managed the impossible and drew one all with Arsenal.

The second occasion was at Chelsea. I took a Dutch boy whose father will feature later in my story. Chelsea were playing a friendly match with an American team starring Johan Cruyff – football lovers will know of him. I took the Dutch boy to his father who was already there and as I walked away, said to an attendant, "Any chance of getting in to see the game?"

"You come with me, sir. He took me to a section of a stand and said, "You sit somewhere there, sir. You may get asked to move because you're in someone else's seat, but there are bound to be a few empties so you'll end up all right."

People came and sat all round me but no one asked me to move. They greeted me as if they thought perhaps they ought to know who I was and I greeted them back. We watched the first half and then a lot of girls in Dutch national costume came amongst us with free refreshments. I was in the midst of a group of butchers and we were being plied with free goodies courtesy of the Dutch meat marketing board.

On neither of these occasions did I let on to my customers that I had seen the match. I just asked all the right questions. The same was true on the third and last occasion I'm going to mention.

I took a carful of people down to Southampton to see the Kirov ballet. Ballet isn't everybody's cup of tea but I'm very fond of it. So I allowed my passengers good time to get inside and then sought and bought a ticket for myself – just six rows behind my passengers. But they never knew that I had seen the ballet, too.

13

Tourists

Our situation in Surrey couldn't have been better. There were a lot of wealthy people in the area who could afford to pay for our services. We were about fifteen miles from London and almost equidistant between Heathrow and Gatwick airports.

Inevitably a lot of our work involved taking people to the airports and meeting them on their return. And we had all the usual experiences: planes diverted from one airport to another were perhaps the worst. The only time I ever failed to get to an airport was the morning after the hurricane in 1989. There was simply no way through, but when I got home and phoned I found that the planes were not flying anyway!

We had people arriving home and finding that they had picked up the wrong suitcase – which meant another airport trip. And on one occasion I took a Dutch businessman to Heathrow with instructions to meet him in the evening. Later I had a phone call asking me to pick up his passport and take it with me to the airport. He came through in the usual way and never needed his passport. When I asked him how he had managed he said, "Oh, I had picked up my wife's passport by mistake so I used that."

There are two particular tourists that I thought I would write about. The first was a US Senator's widow. She had family in the USA but she also had a daughter and grandchildren living in Surrey. She and her daughter loved each other dearly, but they couldn't get on with one another. Once a year the mother would come over from the States to see her daughter and her grandchildren. Twenty-four hours after her arrival her daughter would ring me.

"Can you come and take my mother off my hands. We are driving one another crazy."

So I would. At the end of our time together I usually took her back to her daughter, and the following day her daughter would take her to the airport and say farewell.

The first time I drove her she asked me to drive her 'right round the coast of Cornwall'. I took her literally, with the result that we drove through plenty of narrow Cornish lanes. She grumbled that she couldn't see anything and I explained that that is one of the features of the west country; the countryside is so very beautiful but if all you do is drive you can only expect to catch glimpses. All we did WAS drive. She hardly got out of the car at all.

In those days you could still drive through Polperro. With a long car there was one spot where you needed to do a bit of careful inching forward, then inching back until you were in position to continue forwards. I did what was necessary and there came a sigh from the back of the car:

"I guess I don't need to question your driving skills any more."

So I had passed and would be used again! I don't remember where we stopped that first night. I dropped her at the best hotel in town and then went off to find a bed and breakfast for myself. The following morning I learned that the room the hotel had given her was not good enough and had had to be changed once? twice? It was to be a pattern repeated everywhere we went. The rooms were never good enough and hotel staff were always happy to see the back of her.

We drove on to Land's End and here she did get out of the car. To look at the view? Well, no. To visit the post office and buy some 'postal cards' and stamps. And then she said to the lady behind the counter in the post office:

"Could I borrow your sponge for the stamps. You never know whose hands have touched them."

The lady's hackles rose but she passed the sponge through.

After we had completed our tour of Cornwall I took her to one of London's best known hotels. The room had to be changed, of course. I don't remember in detail the rest of the week but there were two trips I DO remember. I never knew in advance where we were going, but I arrived to pick her up one afternoon and she said:

"I'd like to see a road where the trees meet one another over the road and form a kind of tunnel."

I told her we would have to go well out of London. That was OK, so we had a lovely drive in the Surrey countryside. She saw what she wanted and I had a thoroughly good time.

The next day she wanted to go to Lavenham in Suffolk.

I had never been there but I spent a minute or two with a map and we set off. She must have read about it somewhere and wanted to stay at the famous Swan Inn (yes, she did require a change of room). It was a trip for which I was very grateful. Lavenham really is pretty special with its magnificent medieval timber houses. While she stayed in the Swan Inn I had the chance of a really good wander round, and years later had the opportunity to go again and take my wife.

I was to drive this lady year after year for several years, and was often to be very frustrated because it was impossible to plan anything. She would sit in the back of the car shuffling papers around until something caught her eye and then she would say, "Let's go so and so." We would criss cross the country, doubling back on ourselves in a hopeless chaos of journeys.

I didn't mind the fact that she was wasting her money and adding to mine, but I could have done so much better for her if she had allowed me to. And some of our journeys were utterly crazy.

On one occasion she had decided to DO Wales but we were no sooner in Wales than she wanted to go to Lincoln. So we went to Lincoln.

"Is there anywhere in particular in Lincoln?"

"Yes, the Cathedral. I want to see Magna Carta."

I was feeling frustrated enough to speak my mind:

"There are several copies of Magna Carta, you know. You could have seen it in London and you could have seen it when we passed through Salisbury."

"Oh, really?"

We went into the Cathedral Library. She wasn't interested in the Cathedral itself. And there we asked if she

80

could see Magna Carta. I got hold of a librarian (not physically, you understand) and explained that my companion wished to see their copy of Magna Carta. He turned to her and said:

"I'm afraid that won't be possible. You see, our copy is on tour in the United States. But of course, we do have copies for sale if one of those would interest you."

So she bought her copy of the copy and away we went. She never stopped to look at the Cathedral nor to see what other treasures Lincoln might contain. This was utterly typical. Let me give you two more examples.

One morning I picked her up in London. She wanted to see a herb garden in Lambeth, so we went. We were no sooner there than she discovered that it didn't interest her. "Let's go to Castle Howard."

I hadn't a clue where Castle Howard was but one of my books knew – not very far from Scarborough.

"You do realise how far it is to Castle Howard?"

I gave her an estimate of how long it would take us to get there.

"Oh really? Then let's be on our way."

So off we went to Castle Howard. As so often, I was thankful for my Jaguar 4.2, so comfortable and easy to drive and demanding so little of me. We ate up the miles and I felt as if I could drive for ever without a trace of weariness. Those are dangerous thoughts and I knew it wasn't true. But I've never driven cars that took so little out of you.

That afternoon we arrived safely at Castle Howard and found the café. I left her there for an hour while I glimpsed the glories of the house – surely one of the finest in all England – and I stretched my legs and enjoyed something of the wonder of the grounds. And it was while I was walking that I overheard other people talking and discovered why my client had wanted to come all this way.

I had never watched the television series 'Brideshead Revisited' but apparently it was filmed at Castle Howard, or parts of it were. She wanted to go back to the States and say that she had been there. Yet, when I went to collect her for what was going to be a very long journey back to London, I found that she had never left the café! She saw nothing.

We were on our way again when she had her next bright idea. "Let's go to Oxford."

"We certainly can go to Oxford but if we do you will need to stay the night there."

"We'll go to the Randolph Hotel."

So we did. I was delighted. It cut quite a bit off my journey and I had a son living reasonably close to Oxford. I picked her up the following morning assuming that we were going to explore Oxford, but I ought to have known better. She had done Oxford and we were off to London once more.

The second example is similar but was not nearly so demanding. She wanted to go to Glyndebourne. I explained that there was no way she was just going to arrive and find tickets for the evening performance. But she wanted to go so off we went. We arrived and there was a queue for returned tickets.

"Do you want me to see whether I can get a couple of tickets?"

If she was going to Glyndebourne I wasn't going to miss the chance.

"No," she said. "You go, have a walk, and I'll see if I can buy some postal cards."

When I came back she was sitting in the car.

"Where would you like to go next?"

"What do you suggest?"

This was new. "I'm afraid that it is too late for us actually to go and visit anywhere, but we could drop down to the coast – perhaps to Brighton."

So that's what we did, and had an evening meal in a hotel overlooking the sea before driving back to London. She was quite content. She could tell her friends back in the States that she had been to Glyndebourne. But though she had no interest in opera, the show about Mozart and Salieri was playing in London and she felt she couldn't miss it, so one night the two of us went – another tick in my box of gratitude to her.

The very last time that I drove her she was over here with two young teenage grandchildren from the States and she had decided to have another go at 'doing' Wales from north to south. We arrived in Llandudno and spent the night there. The following morning she asked me if I could find a travel agent's.

At the travel agent's she said, "You take the children off for the morning and I'll see you at lunch-time. They were a very pleasant pair and we spent an enjoyable morning by the sea. When we picked her up she wanted to go to Porthmadog Scenic Railway, so we did. I put them on at one end and picked them up at the other. Apparently the carriages were not very comfortable!

"Now we need to go to Southampton," she said.

"Then I'm afraid we're in for a long drive," I answered, but I didn't quibble. After all, we would have 'done' Wales by the time we got there. We found the hotel the travel agent had booked for her, and before she got rid of me she sent the children off to their room and then explained to me what we were doing.

"I had a change of plan. Of course it has meant that we have had to cut our holiday short, but I thought it would be nice for the kids to go home on the *Queen Elizabeth* instead of flying out of Heathrow."

So I was to pick them up the following morning and take them to the docks.

I asked the man on the door where I could find a reasonable B&B. He told me to park in the hotel car park and pointed to a place up the road: "Number 18, sir. They'll look after you."

I booked in and was told that my room wasn't ready but it would be ready when I needed it. So I left my bag in room 423, a double bedroom with one bed still unmade. Room 423? Yes, it was next to number 75 and beyond that was number 30-something. All of the room numbers had come from other hotels!

I went out for a meal and when I came back my room had obviously been thoroughly cleaned. It wasn't en suite, of course. In the middle of the night I needed to go to the toilet – a toilet in a bathroom. In I went to find my host asleep in the bath! He had given me his room. Happily he didn't wake up while I did what was necessary.

When I went to breakfast I was soon aware that this was no ordinary B&B. The other guests had something about them which marked them out. My times as a chaplain in psychiatric hospitals meant that I felt completely at ease and at home. All of the people here, except the owner, were people who spent time in and out of the local psychiatric hospital. When they were out of hospital they stayed here and when they were too ill to stay here, they went back to hospital. But when they were here they all looked after one another and they paid minimal rent for their rooms. I was given the best breakfast I've ever had in a boarding house, beautifully cooked. And then it was time to pay up and go. I had never asked how much I would have to pay. I had been so thankful to get a room latish in the evening.

"Five pounds sir, and just leave it on the table in the hall."

And so to the docks and home – free again.

14

Beth

Beth was the second American I wanted to tell you about. She couldn't have been more different from the first. She was a gutsy semi-invalid who knew what she wanted to do and where she wanted to go, and who made the most of everything, pushing herself to the limit.

She lived near the Grand Canyon on her own – a divorcée – and had worked in a museum. She was very knowledgeable but not at all wealthy. In fact, at home she managed on her invalidity benefits and her pension. Her ex paid her no maintenance at all – except. . .

Once a year he called by and gave her a wad of dollar bills. As soon as she had them she booked a coach tour in the British Isles because she 'just lurved' this country. But of course, coach tours don't really always take you where you want to go and they don't give you long enough in any one spot. I mean, just imagine, a semi-invalid leaving her tour to travel by boat for a one day trip to the Scillies!

She was on her way back to the mainland and found herself sitting next to a young woman who had just completed a holiday on the Scillies. The two of them got talking and the young woman learned that although Beth enjoyed her coach tours and made the most of them she did just wish that sometimes. . .

The young woman said, "What you need is someone like my husband. He would take you wherever you wanted to go and stay as long as you liked."

Well, of course, she could never afford that.

The young woman just happened to be my wife. The three of us chatted and Beth went back to London. Towards the end of her stay she had a day spare and she rang us.

"There's a place down in Kent that I would really love to see. It's called Ightham Mote. Do you think you could take me?"

So I did. It is a medieval manor house with a moat. It belongs to the National Trust now but it has got quite an interesting recent history quite apart from its longer story. It is well off the beaten track so not the kind of place most people would get to. But during the First World War an American soldier was out cycling in the Kent countryside and he came across this place. He was captivated.

"One day," he said to himself, "I'm going to come back and buy this place."

He survived the war, went back to the States, but never forgot his dream. Sure enough, the time came when he was able to come to England and buy Ightham Mote and he was the one who gave it to the National Trust.

Beth thoroughly enjoyed herself and so did I. "I would really lurve to have a proper tour with you," she said, "but of course, it would be far too expensive."

I didn't pretend. I told her just how much she would

have to pay me, but then I added, "If we stayed in bed and breakfast places instead of three star hotels, you might save enough to more or less balance out what you pay for your coach tours."

In the end she went back to the USA to pick out all the places she had never seen along with those she wanted to see again. In due course I had a long letter with all the details. I spent a few happy evenings planning a tour that would embrace everything she wanted (planning these things is often as enjoyable as actually doing them). Finally we agreed that she would come over for three weeks and do the tour that I had planned.

We began with Stonehenge, and at my suggestion added Avebury because there you can still walk amongst the stones, touch them and feel your way back in time. And then we were off to Wales because Beth was crazy about castles, so where else would you go?

Our first B&B in Wales was a farm where we had the best Welsh lamb I have ever had in my life. The experience of being on a farm left Beth more than happy to go on using B&Bs wherever we could.

And mostly they were pretty good. On one occasion we found the couple who owned the B&B still busy renovating an old building. Beth had a ground floor room (she always needed that) which was en suite. When we joined one another for dinner she giggled and said, "I've never had a hot water flush toilet before." The couple had got their plumbing wrong.

On another occasion I chose an old Tudor house because I thought Beth would like its age and period. We were welcomed by a Canadian and his Japanese wife and found the Tudor house transformed into a Japanese home.

There was actually only one guest bedroom but they found room for me, up a ladder in the roof.

We spent a good deal of time in Wales visiting castles, many of them well off the beaten track. Always she struggled round, doing her best to make the most of what she was seeing, and always she *knew* about the places we saw and made our visits interesting – but for me the very best thing about these castles came from their strategic positions. The views from the highest points, where Beth couldn't go, were absolutely superb.

From Wales we travelled to the Lake District, just for a couple of days, and then on to Scotland. Here we drove alongside Loch Lomond and headed north to Glencoe and Fort William. Then we followed the coast, crossed to the Isle of Skye, drove all round it and then followed the coast all the way round to John O'Groats. I was in my element. There can't be anywhere in the world more spectacular or more beautiful than parts of the west and north coasts of Scotland. But I did have one amusing, off-putting experience. We were somewhere, no more than a village, on the north coast of Scotland and found a pub. I went in to buy a couple of sandwiches. The landlord was chatting to a local man and paid no attention to me at all.

I'm not very good in pubs or restaurants. I don't like asserting myself. When I was a child my mother sent me to a barber alone for the first time. I sat and waited, and waited, and waited. Eventually the barber said:

"Were you waiting for a haircut, sonny? I thought you were just watching. It's lunch time now but you come back this afternoon and I'll cut your hair."

Here in Scotland I waited for half an hour before the

landlord finally turned to me and said, "Was you wanting something?"

I told him that I would like a couple of sandwiches. He roared out for his wife and went back to his conversation. Fortunately the sandwiches were worth waiting for.

Further east, ski slopes in the mountains seemed to me to mark an ugly human intrusion into a world which had been fairly free of us. On the other hand, the sight of an occasional mountain hare thrilled me to bits.

We came down much of the east coast of Scotland to the borders. I'm not quite sure from memory which order we saw things but I think we visited Lindisfarne and Bamburgh before turning inland to see the ruins of Jedburgh and Rievaulx Abbeys. I suppose today we should just take pleasure in the magnificence of these places and the sheer beauty of their settings. But I always find myself dwelling on the fact that those who had dedicated their lives to 'holy poverty' ended up with such wealth and spent so lavishly while all around them the general population lived in such real poverty and squalor.

We crossed Yorkshire to the Brontë country. My first visit there had been when the boys were small and we were living near Preston in Lancashire. Our local coal merchant took us in his Rover and on the way his exhaust fell off. You can imagine the racket as we roared up and down the hills of Yorkshire. Fortunately I had no such troubles with my Jaguar. She had taken the whole journey in her stride. After three incredible weeks we finally dropped down to Heathrow and said our farewells. I can't describe how wonderful it was to get home and to be with Wendy once more.

15

Reactions

My driving led to quite a lot of the poems which became published in my book *The Sunshine Glances Through*. Here are just five of them. The first was written while I was driving the US Senator's widow; the last, after I got home from driving Beth:

BOARDING HOUSE BREAKFAST

We sit, six islands of silence.

One more male preserve is broken.
There are three men,
three women,
yet nothing has changed.

The silence continues
broken only
by the munching of toast
and the rustle of newspapers

"Mushrooms on the menu this morning."
A cheerful voice,
a muted response
and silence once more.

Are they lonely too,
or half asleep, or is their silence
contentment and peace?

How
    I
       long
           to be home.

DRIVING INTO LONDON
in the early hours of the morning
(Note: Cobbett called London 'the Great WEN'.)

White mist rises from the ground
and the sun peers through the early morning haze
like someone newly wakened
finding it hard to focus and to see.

The Great Wen calls me
from the open spaces of the countryside
to drive along its empty streets
and enjoy its open, barren silence.

In a couple of hours
these streets will be crammed
with buses, cars and taxis
and multitudes of hurrying people.

Tourists will stop and stare
while their cameras click,
taking millions of snaps
that no one will ever want to see.

But the people of the city
hustle, bustle, rush and crush,
careering through life's little day,
will ask no questions – take their pay.

There is no meaning that the mind can fathom.
The man of faith may claim a plan
but most men neither see
nor seek to see a pattern in it all.

These magnificent and ugly stores
in which the whole world buys or steals,
the office blocks and banks and high-rise flats,
the crawling mass of traffic down below.

We simply drive along the streets of life
until the journey's over
and the day is done. Night falls,
and with the darkness, sleep.

THE CHAUFFEUR'S LAMENT

Sitting alone in the darkness,
Standing outside in the cold,
I wonder what makes you nocturnal
And wait 'til the night has grown old.

You asked for the car around midnight
But the clock shows a quarter to two
And I'm keeping awake with a struggle
What on earth are you finding to do?

You've had dinner and speeches and laughter;
You've met Mr Big and his wife;
You hope for a deal in the future
And the City with rumours is rife.

You've swallowed your oysters for starters,
Made a meal of your favourite meat,
And you've downed a whole bottle of champers:
Please, please don't be sick on the seat.

I watch as the guests leave before you
It's important to get things just right
The Royals precede your departure
But us lackeys can stay here all night.

You are coming at last and I greet you,
The weariness all drops away,
With apologies, friendship, good humour,
We drive home and call it a day.

HOME

After my driving day is done
there is a place to which I come
a place of toil, a place of rest,
a place which represents the best
of all that life can give to man –
a place whose name is simply 'home'.

Its contents mostly second-hand,
its furnishings were never grand,
the cast-offs of our families
enrich our home with memories.
Their pictures hang upon the walls
and give us permanent recall.

The garden too holds memories
with plants purloined and growing gifts.
All round the year love's flowers bloom
and dance before the sun and moon.
We wander slowly hand in hand
delighting in our plot of land.

A LITANY OF LOVE AND LONGING

The wind blows wild at Beachy Head
and hikers shelter in the scrub.
O wind bring close my love to me
that we may share this memory.

Round Cornwall's craggy coast I drove
from Looe to Bude by cliff and cove.
O piskies bring my love to me
that we may share this memory.

'Neath Chepstow Castle's massive walls
the Wye ran peaceful in the sun.
O river bring my love to me
that we may share this memory.

On Skye I watched the setting sun
and walked at midnight all alone.
O piper call my love to me
that we may share this memory.

I waded in the sea tonight
at John O'Groats by evening light.
Come like a mermaid – come to me
that we may share this memory.

From Scotland south to Scarborough
and south again to London town.
O bells of Bow ring out for me
that we may share this memory.

The cat curls up beside the fire
and I am home with you once more.
We sit together silently,
take pleasure in our company.

The VW Weekender in use – one of Leslie's favourites.

Another VW camper van owned by Leslie.

Becky, who went everywhere with Leslie.

The Scrase family crest.

The Toyota Auris hybrid
– Leslie and Wendy's latest car.

Leslie's wife Wendy.

Leslie Scrase.

16

The Irish

Perhaps I ought to add a word about the Irish.

I've mentioned that we did a good deal of school work. Carrying 'naughty' children can often be a bit embarrassing. They see someone or something that sets them off. Down goes the passenger window. They wave and shout and their language is often pretty ripe. A driver has to learn how to deal with such behaviour and clamp down on it.

But how do you clamp down on such behaviour when it comes from adults? After too much to drink and a successful day at the races, or after the Irish had beaten England at Twickenham – again – merriment often led to shouting from the minibus, and if there was a response, shouting sometimes led to obscenity.

It wasn't just the Irish. There were one or two others. I remember two in particular – quite well known in their day. And most of it was quite harmless fun. But most of my own problems came from the Irish and from one particular group of them. They were a delight when they

e

were sober, but how I dreaded driving them later on in the day or night. However, it is not of that group of Irishmen that I want to write.

There was one occasion when I had the job of looking after four Irishmen who were over here for a wedding. But they had decided to make a short holiday of their trip. On the first day I collected them from their hotel in Weybridge and asked them where they wanted to go.

"Over the bridge," they said.

So I drove them two miles to the bridge across the river, and over we went.

"Straight on," they said.

And that's how it was for the whole of the three days. I never knew where we were going, but they did. They were going from one pub to another. At each pub they had made arrangements for a room where they could drink (out of hours) and play cards.

We didn't start very early, so we would get to our first pub at lunchtime, and then they would play and drink through the afternoon. Then on to a second pub for two or three hours in the early evening. And finally to a third for a late night session before going back to their hotel. I assisted them to their rooms and then went home myself.

After three days, which became more and more fun as the time wore on, you can imagine the sort of state they were in on the morning of the wedding. I arrived at ten-thirty, just to make sure they were up. There they all were, sitting around a table playing cards, with a drink to chase the blues away. At eleven they decided to go and change into their dress suits – toppers and tails were the order of the day. Three of them managed very well. They had a shower and changed. The fourth got into a bit of a muddle.

He changed and then showered, which made a bit of a mess of his suit. His friends did their best to tidy him up, by which time it was getting a bit late.

We set off for the church and then one of them exclaimed, "Holy Mary, Mother of God! Did you see that?"

The others looked.

"Oh my God. Oh sweet Jesus, we've overdone it this time. Driver, can you see what we can see?"

"What's that?" I asked.

"Did you see that girl leading an elephant by the side of the road?"

Well of course I did. You could hardly miss seeing an elephant could you? But I wasn't letting on.

"I'm afraid I had my eyes on the road," I said.

"Oh dear God. Hurry and get us to the church, driver."

I didn't mention the fact that the circus was in town – just got them to the church as fast as I could.

The bride was just going in, followed by her bridesmaids. My four men completed the procession. I hoped somebody diverted them into pews before they got to the front of the church.

They may have been the last in. They were certainly the first out. We drove back to their hotel, where the wedding reception was to take place. Two of them hurried in to alter all the place names at the tables. One of the others gave me fifty pounds and told me to go to the local hardware shop and buy five metal buckets.

"Five metal buckets?" I queried.

"Exactly," he said. "Five metal buckets."

So I did as he said and brought the buckets back to him.

"That's one for each of us. We shall be able to make plenty of noise at the reception with those."

"But there are only four of you."

"The fifth is for you, to remember us by."

And I have never forgotten them. What's more, I was using the bucket in my garden only yesterday.

You find it all impossible to believe? Yes, you probably do, yet every word of my account is true. All of which goes to show the value of National Service.

While I was in the Navy and playing rugby for one of the Devonport Services teams, as a teetotaller I never had to buy a drink. There would always be an orange juice on the bar for me. The coach would return to each of the officer's homes and I would help them to the door, or even to their bedrooms. Then, with the other ratings, we would be dropped off at Devonport dockyard gates and I would enter with three ratings on each arm! I often thought that was the only reason I was picked to play.

17

The Red Ford Minibus

It was driving tourists, and particularly doing sub-contracted work for a tourist operator, that led us to buy a minibus. In due course changes in the law led me to put some of our drivers, including myself, through a bus driver's test. There was one item in the booklet we read which amused me – but of course you would never get a question on it. No? The day for my test came. The driving part of it was over and then I had to answer a series of questions.

"Your bus is full of passengers and you have to reverse into a cul de sac from the main road. Describe the way you would do it."

Sounds straightforward enough, doesn't it? But I grinned.

"First I would ask all my passengers to disembark and I would ensure that they were all quite safe, and then. . ."

Have you ever known a bus driver ask all of his passengers to disembark while he did a bit of manoeuvring? The only times I was ever asked to disembark were during the war when buses powered from gas containers couldn't get up the hills near Bideford. We would get off and then get back on again at the top of the hill. And the only time I've been driving a bus and stopped to let everyone get off was with a load of mentally handicapped men on the way to Eastbourne. They were desperate for a wee, so we stopped, lined up facing the hedge, and did what was necessary!

Our minibus proved to be very useful and led to a further extension of our business. We began to transport schoolchildren.

Handicapped children were a pleasure to drive but we sometimes had naughty boys and girls too. Some of our drivers had problems with them although I never did. For these we bought a variety of second-hand cars or buses, but just occasionally the demands on our fleet were such that a bunch of the 'naughties' would be driven to school or home in a Jag. You can imagine how they loved that. One of the runs we were sometimes sub-contracted to do was from Cranleigh in Surrey up to Walton on Thames.

I picked some children up in Cranleigh one day, came out from the school and turned left.

"You should have gone the other way."

"Yes, you're right. The other way leads to the main road, but this way will take us through some beautiful countryside and you will get home just as quickly."

I very much doubt if they saw anything of the countryside, but I did. Similarly, I often took people to Gatwick after the motorways were built. I offered passengers a choice of route: motorways or countryside? I often got lucky. The country route took perhaps a quarter of an hour longer but was far more enjoyable and never subject to hold-ups. Of course, when I was on my own I always used the country routes and often stopped off to have a walk in the country. It all helped to make my job a pleasure.

Before I return to the story of the minibus let me tell you about one particular thirteen year old girl. Her parents had divorced and her father had moved with her eighteen miles from her school. I don't know why she wasn't transferred to a local school but instead she was provided with a car to take her to and from her original school. Every morning we would pick her up. Every morning she would insert her tape of Meat Loaf into our player and off we would go. We would drop her at the gates to the school, pick her up in the afternoon, enjoy or endure Meat Loaf again, and she would tell us about her day in school. This went on for a month, and then we had a phone call from Social Services: why were we not taking the girl to school?

Apparently, every day after we dropped her off at school, she watched us out of sight and then walked the half a mile to her mother's house. Having spent the day with her mother, she made sure that she was back at school waiting for us when we arrived to pick her up. Sadly, I don't know the end of her story. She was a very pleasant girl to drive. I hope she has done well with her life.

The value of school work was that it gave us an assured income, but there were disadvantages to it as well. First of all, you had to quote rock bottom prices to get it. And secondly, you were subject to the whims of local authorities who constantly changed the rules. It was one change in their rules that forced us to take tests as bus drivers. I would have been quite happy about that except for the fact that schoolteachers were allowed to drive the same number of pupils from their schools in their own minibuses without taking the test.

But it was another sudden change of rule which caught us quite a wallop and led to my decision to phase out school work altogether. I had quoted for a new run, got it, and bought a brand new little Daihatsu six-seater for the run. It was perfect for the job. And then, out of the blue, came the dictat that vehicles for school runs had to have engines of 1500cc or over. Several of our vehicles, including the Daihatsu, had smaller engines. The best I could get out of the County was one term's grace in which to replace them all.

But I have digressed. I began this chapter with the story of our minibus. Experience years before of a holiday in Devon in a minibus led us to use our own minibus for another holiday, this time to Scotland.

We took all the rear seats out and replaced them with an old kitchen cupboard which had been relegated to the garden shed. We took a small Calor gas stove and we put a mattress on the floor of the van. So, we had an almost perfect camper van. It's true that Wendy sometimes felt a bit embarrassed when we pulled into a campsite next to a luxurious van that was virtually a second home, but we had fitted some rough and ready curtains so our neighbours weren't able to look inside and envy our luxury.

The van took us to Scotland for the first of a number of wonderful holidays there. But not long after we had returned, and it had reverted to its normal use, our driver rang us up one morning and told us that it had been stolen. Nor was it ever recovered.

But I had been reading about a firm in East or West

Grinstead who converted a VW van into something called a Weekender. In fact, they went further and provided a Weekender that could double up as a minibus. We bought one and found it one of the most valuable vehicles we ever had. It was good enough to satisfy business customers going to Ascot or to the Farnborough Air Show, or Twickenham, or similar events. It was ideal for one of our school runs. And in Weekender mode it was perfect as a motor caravan for more holidays, including holidays in Scotland. It was one of our all time favourite vehicles – certainly one of Wendy's all time favourites.

When we retired to Dorset I made the mistake of leaving it with the family to whom I had given our business. The arrangement was temporary, but when it finally came back to us it was in a sorry state and then cost a bomb to bring it up to scratch again. Added to which, we were growing older and finding floor level cupboards a bit of a problem. However, when I traded it in for an ordinary second-hand camper van, we weren't very happy with the replacement and finally decided that our camping days were over; although I went on hankering for a van for years.

But I have jumped well ahead of myself. As you will have gathered, our business had grown and branched out in a variety of directions. Our core business was still the work done with our three Jaguars/Daimler Sovereigns. (The two cars were identical.) And it was with those that we did all of our business work. Most of our drivers were self-employed part-timers and some of them were supplementing the benefits they were on!

As I've already mentioned, it is amazing how wealthy people grow angry about people living on benefits. I remember once driving an advertising whizz kid home one night. What had we been talking about? I've no idea, but he said, "I've never had to worry about money in my life."

And I thought, "Except when we were in India I don't ever remember a time in my adult life when I didn't have to worry about money."

That was not to change until after we had retired. But if that was true for me, how much more true was it for my drivers on benefits and prepared to do anything to make ends meet. They were, all of them, decent hard-working people but for one reason or another they couldn't find full-time work. And the wealthy begrudged them the help the state was giving, while they themselves were fiddling their expenses, sometimes on a massive scale.

Our society has been irreparably damaged by greed of one kind or another. In the post-war years there was genuine idealism and the gap between rich and poor shrank as we strove to pull together as one nation and to steadily improve the lot of the poor. But working people became too greedy and wanted too much too soon, all of which led to the chaos of the 1970s and the reaction under Margaret Thatcher which opened the flood-gates for the greed of the rich, and led directly to the troubles of the present day when the rich grow richer and the poor begin to struggle again.

One day in 1994, I was driving home from Heathrow after dropping a businessman at the airport and suddenly I felt, "I don't want to do this any more."

I came home and told Wendy how I felt and soon afterwards we put our house on the market, but it was to take us two years to sell. Perhaps it really was time to move on. I was beginning to have nightmares.

18

The Nightmare

Do you ever have nightmares?

I used to have them as a child – two in particular. I had a toy cupboard and in one of them I would open the door to the cupboard and find all my toys guarded by a crocodile or a lion. I couldn't get to them. But much more common was one I'm told a lot of children have. In mine, the walls of the bedroom turned into balls and rolled towards me getting bigger all the time and closer, closer until. . .

And then for years I never had a nightmare – not until I was in my early forties and my first marriage was drawing to a close. But it was twenty years later, towards the end of my time with Alpha Cars, that nightmares began again. Always they would involve the loss of a car at a crucial time. I'd be at Heathrow with customers walking to the car park and I'd find I couldn't remember where I'd parked my car. Or I would have taken people to London, parked and gone for a walk, and when I came back the car was gone.

107

It was some years after we had moved down here to Dorset when I had an incredibly detailed nightmare. I suppose it was because we were visiting Surrey and London again. I really hate it when I have to go to London.

I knew that I was having a nightmare. That seems strange for a start. It was one of the nightmares from my chauffeuring days, so I knew the way it would go. The details would he different but the end result would be the same. I knew all this but it didn't ease the tension or reduce the sense of panic.

I had to collect my solicitor customer. He was exceptionally demanding, and yet in one respect he was also one of the best customers I had. If he asked me to collect him at eleven o'clock outside his office, he would be there on the dot of eleven. In London that kind of customer deserves all the medals that are going.

For some strange reason Wendy was with me as I drove up to town. Why? She never came with me. It just wasn't the thing to do. Yet, as I drove the Jag quietly westwards along Fleet Street, there she was beside me. She had no business to be there. My solicitor would not be pleased.

Just before Chancery Lane, Fleet Street was closed off. It hadn't been closed two days earlier when I had driven my solicitor to his office opposite the Royal Courts of Justice.

Typical.

And I had timed my arrival to a nicety. It was no use trying detours. They would make me late. The only thing to do was to park the car, run around the blockade to the office and bring the solicitor back.

"Come on," I cried.

Why did I take Wendy? It would have been quicker if I

had left her in the car. We circled the blockade to find that a hotel had been built right across the road. It hadn't been there two days before. But this was London. Anything could happen in London. Should we run back a bit, cut down to the river and come up from there to the Strand? Or should we run up Chancery Lane, round the back of the Courts of Justice and down again?

Neither. There wasn't time. We raced into the hotel but there seemed to be no way through to the back. We ran down a corridor and into a bedroom. A partition separated the room from the back half of the hotel. Wendy was onto the bed and over the partition in a flash. I stopped to take my shoes off before getting onto the bed. It's the sort of thing you do if you've been properly brought up. Oh dear. No, I'm not suggesting that Wendy wasn't properly brought up. I'm just. . . oh, never mind. Anyway, I took my shoes off and climbed over the partition.

Idiot! I had left my shoes behind. Back to the top of the partition. Two Chinese cleaners were in the room. Thank goodness. I pointed to my shoes.

"Could I have my shoes please?"

They looked at me quizzically. These strange Englishmen. One of them took off her shoes and offered them to me.

"No. Not *your* shoes. My shoes please." I pointed again.

The other girl took off her shoes and offered them to me. I screamed, "*My* shoes, please!"

A manageress came in. "What's going on?"

I scrambled down, grabbed my shoes and fled, leaving the Chinese girls giggling delightedly. But we still couldn't get out. We were in a lounge overlooking gardens. The armchairs were full of elderly people as if the hotel were a nursing home.

"How do we get into the gardens?" I asked.

"You can't get out until you've paid." The response was like a chorus.

"But we aren't staying here."

"You can't get out until you've paid."

I don't know how we did get out, but we did. We ran through the garden and on and on as if it were one of the avenues of trees in Bushy Park. And then we were on the Strand and outside my customer's office. He had gone, of course. It was ten minutes past eleven. He wouldn't wait ten minutes. He would probably never use me again.

Disconsolate, we walked down to the river. We weren't going through that hotel again. From the river we made our way back up to Fleet Street to the spot where we had left the car.

I knew what we would find before we got there. The only thing I didn't know was whether it had been stolen or towed away. It was always one or the other.

When I woke I wasn't sorry that our stay was over. We would be on our way back to Dorset later that day.

19

The Police

I haven't had many dealings with the police. When I have, our relationship has usually been pretty good. Perhaps I have been helped by my upbringing. I was always taught to look upon the police as my friends.

And yet in adult life I have always been a bit timid in the face of authority. It wasn't always the case. At school, with a very authoritarian headmaster, after a plentiful succession of beatings I learned to stand up to him and got away with murder.

I date my adult timidity from my days in the Navy. When you are shouted at morning, noon and night, and told in no uncertain terms that you are one of a group of men who are a 'shower of shit', it doesn't do very much for your confidence.

For a very long time after the Navy I was uncomfortable in the presence of anybody in a uniform. One of the reasons I have rarely travelled out of this country is my dread of customs officers. Even though I have done nothing wrong I hate having to deal with them. Nor was it only men and women in uniform. Bank managers, solicitors, doctors even: all of them had a wealth of knowledge and experience that gave them authority over me and filled me with dread. And yet, in spite of that, even in the Navy there were times when I bucked my normal fears and 'tried it on' and got away with it. Looking back I can't credit some of the things I did.

And three times in my driving years the police got up my nose to such a degree that I became quite obstreperous. On all three occasions I had a police car behind me. On the first I drove right through Woking from one end to the other and the police car was behind me all the way. As we left the speed restriction (30? 35?) the police pulled me over:

"Can't you see what a tail-back you've caused?"

"And if I'd speeded up you would have done me for speeding." That dealt with that.

On another occasion I was driving through Twickenham, again with a police car behind me, and the lights changed. I was a bit close to them but clapped on my brakes and stopped. After the lights I was pulled over and two officers got out of the police car. The driver came back to me. She was fuming.

"Don't you realise how powerful your brakes are? I very nearly ran into your rear. You need to watch what's behind you."

"I knew what was behind me. And if I hadn't stopped you would have done me for crossing a red light."

"Well you ought to be more careful."

I didn't take it any further and they got back into their patrol car and drove off without indicating. I didn't bother to follow and tell them off.

The third occasion was at two o'clock in the morning. I had a couple of Americans in the back of the car. A blue light began flashing behind me so I pulled over and the police got out.

"Why did you swerve back there?"

"I don't remember swerving but if I did there must have been a good reason."

"And why didn't you stop when you saw our blue light."

"I did. It was because of your light that I pulled in here."

"Our blue light has been flashing for a good half a mile."

"You were driving very close to my tail. If you like to get into my driving seat and look in the mirror you'll see that your blue light is invisible at such close quarters."

The other policeman said, "Would you mind just blowing into this bag for us, sir?"

"Since I'm teetotal I wouldn't mind at all." So I blew into their bag, we got back into our cars and drove away.

One of the Americans said, "Poor chaps. At two o'clock in the morning they've got nothing else to do."

I think perhaps I was wise not to mention that I'd driven their chief constable a couple of weeks earlier.

20

Book Keeping

Before we went to India the church gave us a three day course in double-entry book-keeping and office management. It was probably the most useful course I ever went on in my life.

Both as manager of Gold Star and as owner of Alpha Cars it meant that I was able to keep the books without paying anybody else. After all, it was all pretty simple.

Towards the end of our time with Alpha Cars we had inspections both from the Inland Revenue and from the VAT people (Customs and Excise). The VAT people took two days over it. They all went away happy, which left me happy too.

Accounts then were kept simply with a cash book and ledger. About five years before we finished, someone came to try to sell me a computer – about £1000 if my memory serves me correctly. I asked him what he thought five cash books and five ledgers would cost? So we didn't buy a computer and twenty-five years later I'm still managing to live without one.

But I'm told that it is compulsory now to do your VAT on a computer.

21
Great Benefits
With Little Thanks

I must have been in my early teens when I first began to
be aware of words in the Methodist Covenant Service that
have lived with me all my life: 'We have taken great
benefits with little thanks.'

There have certainly been 'great benefits'. To take just
one example: look anywhere you like in our house and
you will see things which used to belong to somebody else
– usually somebody in one of our families. So how do we
say thank you.

When I was a schoolboy we used to say "T.V.M." –
"thank you very much." But when you've said that, you
have said just about all that you can say in English, and if
you try to say more it soon begins to look and feel as if you
are over-doing things. How do you say more when the
language just won't let you?

When we went to India, back in the 1960s, and began to
be introduced to the local language, Telugu, one of the first
questions I asked was, "How do I say 'thank you' in

Telugu?" The answer I was given was that you can't. There is no word for thank you. The trouble is, I'm no linguist. In fact, you would be complimenting my linguistic skills if you said: "Les is no linguist."

But I persisted: "You MUST be able to say thank you." Eventually I was told that I could try using a word that sounded like 'wunderlumulu', so I did but I never knew whether that really said what I wanted to say.

When I began to write this book it wasn't long before I began to be aware of the huge debts of gratitude I owe to a host of other people. I began to scribble names and to think of people whose names I never knew or don't remember. It was hopeless. Where do you end? There are so many. *You* try it for your own lives.

But if it was hopeless, not least because there was no way that I could write about them all, it was also a wonderfully uplifting experience. I was bringing back to mind people I hadn't thought about in years and the sheer cumulative effect of thinking of all those people drove home once again what a very lucky little boy – oh, all right, old man – I've been.

I can't write about them all, but I can perhaps write about some of the people who have brought me 'great benefits' in my life with cars. And if I do that, I should probably begin with my father who taught me the joy of driving quietly and smoothly, without hurry, through the quieter lanes and roads of the English countryside. And who, at the other end of his life, sold me his last car, a Triumph 2000, which became a very useful addition to our fleet.

Over the years other people, customers, sold me cars instead of trading them in. Several of my Jaguars came to

116

me that way. I thought a Rolls was going to come, too. The owner promised me first refusal but must have forgotten all about his promise when the time came. As it happens I wasn't sorry. I had driven it and preferred driving my Jags and Daimlers, and it would have had a very limited usefulness.

There was one of my brothers, and there were other customers, who helped me with the loan of money and there was one who flatly refused to take the final repayment or any interest.

But I must go back in time: it was my first father-in-law who taught me to double-de-clutch. And it was while I was driving that 1934 Austin 7 that I experienced some lovely hospitality.

I was driving through Sherborne on my way to London one Sunday night and I stopped to go to the little Methodist chapel there. Before I was allowed to continue on my journey a couple took me home with them for supper. A similar thing happened one Sunday morning in Reading, and happily I was to meet the couple who looked after me that day on a couple of other occasions too.

I could go on and on about the hospitality I've received in my lifetime – perhaps most significantly in India where people who had nothing to give, gave all that they could. And later on some of my customers were wonderfully hospitable too. There was one lady who had every reason not to be hospitable!

The first time I drove her was in the winter, from Surrey to London. We had hardly set off when we came to a T-junction. I slowed carefully but I didn't stop. In fact, I couldn't stop. We slid quietly across the T-road and stopped with our nose in the hedge opposite! In spite of that, she allowed me to continue the journey.

As it happened, both of us were involved with the same 'Riding for the Disabled' organisation, although at the time of that journey we didn't know it. We found out at the AGM when I was in the chair and she and her husband were on the front row!

That led to an occasion when we had a meeting in their home where I spilled coffee on their brand new carpet. You see what I mean about not deserving hospitality or generosity?

Often, driving one member of a family led on to driving others in the same family, and when you do that over a number of years you often build lasting friendships, and you have the pleasure of seeing children grow up and even in sharing in their lives. One of my all time favourites was the mother of adult children, a lady called Mrs Bodkin, who was wonderfully kind both to me and to Wendy. Her daughters were a joy to drive, too – they teased me mercilessly.

There are two others I shall name elsewhere but on the whole I'm going to avoid the naming of names. However, I want to make one other exception. For years I drove a publisher from Finland and came to know his first wife and his first two children well, as well as meeting quite a lot of people from the Finnish community in the London area. They all treated me with immense kindness – and sometimes tested my stamina pretty exhaustively too! How fortunate it is that I have always been teetotal.

But I particularly wanted to mention Markku because he was the one who published the first edition of my book

Coping with Death. Without him it might never have seen the light of day.

All of these people, and all the other people in my life to whom I owe debts of gratitude, made me want to include this chapter in this book.

22

Different and Yet the Same

I had left the church back in 1973. Three years later I joined the British Humanist Association because it seemed to be the least strident non-religious organisation. I read a good deal and found myself in tune with humanist philosophy, and I joined a humanist group in Guildford and made good friends there.

Six weeks after I joined the BHA the General Secretary rang up and said, "With your past experience, could you conduct a funeral for a humanist family in North London?"

At that time there were only about half a dozen people throughout the country taking non-religious funerals. I only know of one other in the London area, still a friend of mine. I went back to my old religious service books and examined the funeral services carefully. What was their shape? What did they contain? What were the service providers trying to achieve? And then I set about quietly considering what a humanist funeral should try to achieve and what it should contain. And how could a non-religious service or ceremony still manage to be inclusive so that religious people attending it would feel included and at home? I had always hated it when clergy or ministers tried to use funerals as an evangelical opportunity, so there was no way that my ceremonies would ever bang a humanist drum!

I took that particular funeral and in due course was called back by the family to conduct another for them. We kept in touch for many years. But that one funeral led me to think that there must be many people who were not members of any organisation but who would welcome an alternative to the services provided by the church. So I picked up my yellow pages and wrote to every funeral director within about ten miles of where I was living.

As a result, from the very beginning of my life with Alpha Cars I had another separate life, a life which was a kind of continuation of the ministry I had had until 1973. It took off very slowly but by the time I was beginning to feel that I'd had enough of my business, I was conducting over a hundred ceremonies a year and I'd had to put in a manager to run the business for me. That manager was a young man with four children. He and his wife proved to be excellent and served us exceptionally well as we moved towards retirement. In the end I decided to give them the business instead of trying to sell it. Financially it was a stupid decision and I'm afraid it didn't work out as I had hoped for them either. Within a couple of years they had run the business into the ground and stripped it of its assets. But that is all water under the bridge.

Because there were so few celebrants about, I sometimes travelled huge distances to conduct funerals.

f

From Surrey I went all over London. One funeral director seemed to be the number one choice for gays and lesbians and I seemed to be his number one choice for gay funerals. It often meant walking quite a tight-rope between the gay community and families. Only once did I have a lesbian funeral – I suspect that it was a mistake! After all, my first name is 'Leslie' and hosts of people confuse Leslie and Lesley. They were a pretty extreme and militant group and it was one of my worst experiences.

On another occasion I had to travel down to Tunbridge Wells; on another to Canterbury; and several times to Brighton – and of course, each journey had to be made twice: once to see the family and once to take the funeral.

Nowadays there are so many celebrants around that so much travelling would be unnecessary.

During the two years it took us to sell our house we had decided that we wanted to live in Dorset. A holiday in our Weekender had led to the decision. We wanted somewhere quiet; somewhere by the sea but still somewhere not too far from our scattered family. They were living in an arc running from Surrey and Sussex through Wiltshire down to Bath and Bristol.

We set off from our home in Surrey down to the coast. We already knew the coast from Brighton east to Dover reasonably well and although we had often enjoyed bits of it, none of it grabbed us or seemed to fit the bill. Wendy was more flexible than I was, conditioned as I was by my evacuation years in North Devon – but North Devon seemed a long, long way away.

Beginning at Bognor, we took a holiday gradually moving westwards. Nowhere took our fancy, although we enjoyed ourselves all through our holiday – nowhere that is until we came to Bridport. We went no further. (Yet we could have done: when we finally packed up to move I found a little booklet I had bought on our minibus holiday in Seaton in East Devon back in the 1970s. It was entitled 'Buying a house in East Devon' – so we had been tempted even then. But we stayed the Dorset side of the border.)

Ultimately we managed to move to Bridport, to Wendy's dream home: a bungalow on the side of a hill with superb views, in a lane of just five properties. Sadly we had overstretched ourselves and other things were to intrude and compound our financial problems, meaning that after seven years we had to move again – but at least we had those seven years, and now as I write, I'm aware that our health would not have allowed us to remain there for ever. It was while we were living there that the last real car sagas of our lives were to run their dramatic course.

Not all that long before we left Surrey, I had the privilege of sharing in the training of a young lady as a celebrant. By this time the British Humanist Association had woken up to the possibilities that celebrants could offer and were beginning to set up an organisation and sketchy training schemes. I went to one of the early ones and was later to become a trainer myself.

When we arrived in Dorset there were no celebrants (apart from one in Yeovil who restricted himself to members of his local Humanist group). Indeed, there were none between Exeter and Bournemouth, although both of those places had celebrants. But it meant that I had a huge empire to tap. Like Great Britain, I have gradually and willingly shed chunks of my empire as more and more celebrants (some of them trained by myself) have come on stream. I've been very lucky. They have gradually taken the more distant parts of my empire until I am, at the time of writing, left only with my own local area. Why have I given up WILLINGLY? At one point I was doing 250 ceremonies a year – far too many.

It is incredible how lucky I have been. The first new celebrant to arrive took over the Yeovil area from me and the second, a lady I helped to launch, took over East Devon. But with a smaller empire I found myself busier than before. I didn't have to say 'no' so often now that my work was more concentrated. And so it has gone on – new celebrants nibbling away at the extremities of my empire and always leaving me busier than before until the most recent three arrived to rob me of Dorchester, Weymouth and Portland. So, at long last, with only my immediate area left, I am down to about one hundred ceremonies a year.

Now that I am back down to just over 100, life seems to me to be just about perfect. I still have a purpose in life but we also have time for ourselves.

But all this is really a digression – I seem to digress pretty often. Perhaps I'm beginning to grow old? We must return to the final stages of my saga with cars and a few more examples of why I have called this book *Driven Crazy*.

Among the mistakes I made when I gave Alpha Cars away was my decision to lend our VW Weekender for two years to the firm. Instead we began our life in Dorset with an elderly Toyota that both of us enjoyed. With my empire taking me to Exeter, Taunton, Salisbury, Poole and Bournemouth, and with family to visit spread around that great arc I mentioned, it was clear that we would continue to do a fair mileage. And in those days both Wendy and our dog Becky came everywhere with me.

23

Fun, Fantasy and Flummery

Most of the stuff I wrote while I was a minister of religion ended up in the rubbish bins – something which upset one of my daughters at the time, but I never regretted getting rid of it all.

And then for a very long time I neither had the time nor the energy to do any writing. Then grandchildren began to come along and took me back to my own childhood and I began writing once more. But it was not until we came down to Dorset that my writing really took off again. Some of it was serious and some of it not so serious.

It was in my fantasy *It's Another World* that I found myself writing about two tiny Daihatsu camper vans. It might be fun to turn to those stories once again.

It all began one evening. We had been to Cogden Beach in the afternoon, just a few miles away, and after our tea and TV news, we were just settling down for the evening. Quite suddenly, out of the blue, Wendy said:

"Our car's getting terribly rusty."

"Yes it is," I said, "but you love that old car."

It was true. It was an old turquoise Toyota Carina, an automatic that had cost us £800. We had driven it, and driven it, mile after trouble free mile. Goodness knows how old it was now but it was well into its second hundred thousand miles.

And it was getting pretty rusty.

"Perhaps it's time we thought about a replacement," she said sadly.

"If we do, we could do with a small camper van."

"It would have to be a very small camper van," she said.

You know how it is with these things. They're like having your appendix out or having your hip done. As soon as the subject is broached you meet everybody else who has had the same things dealt with. We had no sooner broached the subject of a camper van than I found a firm just beginning a promotion for a baby Daihatsu Hijetta. They would actually come and show us one. And they did.

I knew we were sunk as soon as I saw the salesman: young, blond and bronzed, and in spite of all that, a very pleasant man to talk to. He didn't push for a sale. He simply showed us round the vehicle and let it sell itself. It was incredibly small but there was an amazing amount in it. We were hooked.

So it was farewell Carina and hello Hijetta. Wendy named it 'Pip Squeak' straight away and inwardly she was smiling all the way from the bank. She knew what men are like with cars – even such a tiny little vehicle as this.

For a while I was like a child with a new toy. Come to that, Pip Squeak WAS rather like a toy. But then November arrived.

I don't like the noise of fireworks. I never did, not even as a boy. But we would sit in our conservatory, high above the town, and look down and watch the fireworks fly high up into the night sky and then burst in all their glory, and we didn't hear a sound.

It was the day after bonfire night that I had to go to Axminster. I don't remember the reason why but Wendy chose not to come. That was unusual for a start. She comes everywhere with me so that we can enjoy those conversation-free chats of ours. Luckily as it turned out, I left Becky at home too.

I set off in little Pip Squeak along the A5 past Charmouth. I climbed over the top of the hills north of Lyme Regis and into Devon. Before long we had another climb up Raymond's Hill. Pip Squeak was a bit slow when it comes to climbing so I was very conscious of everything behind me and wondering how I could best let it pass.

There seemed to be a fair bit of mist behind me on the climb, which was strange because it was a lovely fine day. No, it wasn't mist. But surely my exhaust shouldn't be smoking, belching out stuff like that? It was a new car, for goodness sake. I thought perhaps I ought to take a look so I pulled into the first layby I came to. As I did so, a car raced past with a lady leaning out of the passenger window pointing at my car. How rude! Some people! Make a fuss about the least little thing. I got out and strolled round to have a look.

Oh, wow!

Pip Squeak was on fire. I pulled out my fire extinguisher and before long I had the fire not just under control but out. Then I had a look around and discovered that I was in luck – there was a telephone box not far up the road. I phoned the RAC and in due course they sent me a giant pickup truck to take us to the Daihatsu garage.

Jim the foreman had a good look at the poor little thing. He sucked in through his teeth. "Can't understand that," he said. "It's new, isn't it?"

"Brand new," I said.

"Never known such a thing to happen before," he said. "You haven't been playing with fireworks, have you?"

"No," I answered.

"We'd better have a proper look at it," he said. "So you'll need something to get you home."

"Yes I will," I answered.

"We can arrange that for you," he said, and they lent me a car which I could keep until they had sorted out poor little Pip Squeak.

It was a couple of days later that he rang me up.

"We've had a good look at your vehicle and we've no idea why she caught fire. I've never known such a thing to happen before. We'll repair it, of course, free of charge."

"I don't think I'm going to feel safe driving her again if you haven't been able to find anything wrong."

"No," he said. "Perhaps I'd better have another look."

It was another couple of days before he rang me again.

"We've repaired your car," he said.

"And have you found out what caused it to catch fire?"

"There was oil on the exhaust," he said.

"She's a brand new vehicle," I said.

"Yes," he said. "Perhaps I'd better have a word."

"I'd be grateful if you would."

Half an hour later he rang again.

"I've had a word," he said.

"And?"

"And we'll give you a new vehicle to replace the one that caught fire."

"Excellent," I said.

"Only there's a snag."

Isn't there always.

"Go on."

"There aren't a lot of these kind of vehicles about."

"That's true."

"And we'd rather like our vehicle back."

"So?"

"We'd like you to take your vehicle. Then you can either wait until the makers supply us with another one, which could be some time, or you could drive across to their factory and then they'll give you one straight away."

"Fine. Where's their factory?"

"Sussex."

"Sussex!" I exclaimed.

He was careful to make no comment, and after a pause I said, "OK. I'll go to Sussex and fetch my new car myself."

So we made arrangements for me to pick Pip Squeak up, and when I did we made arrangements for the trip to Sussex. I wasn't too happy having to drive there in a car which had caught fire for no discernible reason, but what else could I do?

24

A Trip to Sussex

Quite a lot of our family live in Sussex and Surrey. Given my surname, that's not surprising. It's a Sussex name. The family tradition from a long time ago is that we came over with the Danes. But there is no sign of us in the Domesday Book. My own guess is that we came over with the Normans But we can't be sure. However, we have certainly been in Sussex from the time of Edward 1st. And later on obtained a crest.

We can't trace my own branch of the family back as far as that. We have been traced back to the early 1500s, living in Cuckfield, and from that time we were normally tenant farmers living in the Haywards Heath and Burgess Hill areas. We have spread a little from Sussex. There is a fair group of us in the South West, in Gloucestershire and Bristol. And when I first took an interest in the subject ALL of the few Scrases in Canada came from our branch line. (My book *Some Sussex and Surrey Scrases* is long since out of print.)

Given these facts, I thought that Wendy would love to

come with me to collect Pip Squeak Mark 2. Then we could spend a few days doing the rounds and showing off our new camper van.

"Not on your life," she said. "You needn't think I'm going all that way in a car that bursts into flame."

I did my best to persuade her but I have to admit I did see that she had a point. So I set off alone and not without apprehensions of my own.

I have never kept so close an eye on the rear of a car in all my fifty years of driving. But Pip Squeak drove beautifully. She was faultless. It was as if she wanted to make quite sure that I knew what a fool I was to trade her in for another. She really did drive well. But it was no use. The decision had been made.

So we drove to Sussex, and Pip Squeak the second was waiting for me, all ready with a full tank of petrol. But there was more. They presented me with a huge bouquet of flowers and a bottle of whisky – I was overwhelmed: such kindness, such generosity. How could anything ever go wrong again?

My road took me past Lewes and up to Haywards Heath, where the very first known members of my own branch of the family lived all those centuries ago. And it was there that I noticed the red light.

No, not traffic lights and not a pedestrian crossing. A red light inside the car on the dashboard. It couldn't be. It just wasn't possible.

But it was.

I pulled off the main road into a residential side road. I checked the owner's manual. It was all very clear and straightforward, yet I didn't seem to be able to find out what was wrong. Was anything wrong at all? I switched

131

on the engine again and the little red light came on again.

So I took a careful note of precisely where I was and went to phone the RAC.

"Again?" said the telephonist. "You haven't caught fire again?"

"No," I said. "I haven't caught fire again. I'm in a brand new vehicle, only collected today, and a little red warning light is showing."

"Which little red warning light, sir?"

"That's just the trouble," I said. "I can't make out which light it is."

He sighed. "Where are you, sir?"

I told him precisely where I was.

"We'll be with you in about an hour, sir. Just wait with your vehicle."

So I settled down to wait. How fortunate I was that I was able to make myself a cup of coffee and generally look after myself. There are times when it really is helpful having a camper. Two hours later I rang the RAC again.

"Yes sir. He's on his way but he seems to be having some difficulty locating you."

So again, I told the man precisely where I was and went back to wait. I decided to have a nap. The nice thing about a camper is that your bed is already there, so I stretched out and two hours later, when I came to, it really seemed to me as though the RAC ought to have arrived. I went back to the phone box.

"We are so sorry, sir, we don't seem to be able to find you."

"But I've given you my location twice."

"Yes sir, but we can't find you. Two of our patrols have failed to find you."

"But I'm in an old residential road off the A272."

"Yes sir, so you said. But we can't find you."

I was beginning to get the message. "Have you got a map?" I said.

"It's on the screen in front of me, sir."

"Very well. Can you find the A272 as it comes into Haywards Heath from the east?"

"Yes sir."

My question might have treated him like an idiot but he was determined to remain polite.

"Please take me through Haywards Heath on your map and name every turning off the A272 to the left." I was being extraordinarily calm and patient you see.

So was he. He did just as I asked and then he suddenly stopped and said, "There seems to be a bit of a gap in the map. Excuse me, just a minute, sir." He brought the same map up on another telephonist's screen and found the same gap. He tried a third screen. "That's funny, sir. All our screens seem to have the same problem. I'll just fetch a Sussex atlas."

I waited.

"I've got it, sir. I shan't be a moment."

There was a long pause. A very long pause. And then he said, "That's strange. The page is missing."

"Old Maud," I said, thinking that I was saying it to myself. (Old Maud was a witch who plagued us for years, as readers of *It's Another World* will know. Thanks to our dog Becky and a rowan tree we finally put an end to her pranks.)

"Pardon sir?"

133

I laughed mirthlessly. "It's nothing. Just something I say when I feel like swearing."

"Oh. Yes I suppose you must feel a bit frustrated sir."

"Look," I said. "Ask one of your patrolmen to drive along the A272 through Haywards Heath from east to west. And ask him to check every single side road off to the left."

"Yes sir. I'll do that sir, right away. If you like to wait by your vehicle sir."

So I went back and made another cup of coffee.

An hour and forty minutes later the patrolman arrived. "I'm afraid we've had a bit of a job finding you, sir," he said brightly.

I wasn't feeling too bright I'm afraid, but it was pointless making a scene. So I waited until he asked, "Now what seems to be the matter?"

So I told him and I showed him the red light. At least it still came on.

"This is a new vehicle sir."

"Brand new. I only picked it up today."

"So it's still under warranty."

"Yes, of course."

"Then I'd better not touch it. I'll send a pickup truck."

Suddenly my patience snapped. "No," I said.

"But that's all I can do, sir. He'll take you wherever you want to go."

"It has taken you five hours and forty minutes to find me. Do not send a pickup truck. Fetch one."

"Well, I don't know. . ."

"Fetch one."

He took out his phone and rang headquarters. They authorised him to do as I asked and twenty minutes later he was back with the pickup truck and we set off on the long trip home. Damn that witch.

We left Pip Squeak 2 at the garage with Jim, and the pickup driver took me home. He turned into the entrance to our lane and gasped.

"Do I have to take you down there?" he asked. "It's so. . ." I'm not sure what he was going to say but I spoke for him: "Narrow," I said. "Drop me off here, and thanks for all your help."

I walked the last few hundred yards home wondering what on earth I was going to do about Old Maud. Damn her.

Wendy and Becky were both full of consolation. Nothing can raise the spirits of the depressed more quickly than the utter devotion of a dog and whatever it is that comes nearest to that from a wife. By the time Jim rang the following morning I was almost back to my normal happy self.

"Hello sir, your car's ready."

"Oh good. What was wrong?"

Nothing sir. It was just a faulty warning light, that's all. You can collect the car whenever you like. There'll be no charge, of course.

So that was that. We now had a faultless new car and thanks to the barometer it wasn't long before we had a chance to try her out properly.

(And if you're not into witches and things, the substance of this chapter, including the long long wait, is true.)

25

The Barometer

What on earth has a barometer to do with a book about cars?

Quite a bit actually. In one of the earlier chapters I said that I wasn't going to name any of the famous people I'd driven. But sometimes customers became friends. Three of those were Sue and her parents. In fact, Sue is a very special friend to both of us to this day.

Sue had another friend called Iris and once a week I used to take her to visit an elderly aunt of hers. The aunt was in a nursing home and the two women lived about ten miles from one another. It is amazing how many different ways you can find of travelling ten miles if you've a mind. I worked quite hard at making those journeys enjoyable and varied. When the old aunt died, Iris gave me the barometer as a thank you.

I brought it home and set it up in our porch. It looked just right and I was proud of it. It was old but more important than that, it was a beautiful piece of work. I'm not a man for antiques generally, not unless they really are handsome. This was, even if it was faded and not working. But there in that porch it looked just right. And then we moved to Dorset!

The trouble was it didn't look just right when we moved. We had just the right spot for it, that wasn't the problem. The problem was that in its new home in our hall it cried out for a spot of attention. It needed to be stained again, and it wanted to work. You could see it did. Yet Wendy had never mentioned it before. It was most irritating just as I was getting into my book.

"Well?" she said.

"Oh we'll get it fixed sometime."

"When?"

And then I had a brainwave. Years ago I drove some American tourists who were staying in London. There were a number of places they wanted to go, not because they were interested but because they thought they should, and they liked being driven in the countryside. I must confess, I was surprised when they asked me to take them to Bristol. Bath, yes. Everyone asked to go to Bath, often taking in Salisbury and Stonehenge on the same day. But Bristol?

"We want to buy a barometer," they said, and they showed me an article they had taken from an American tourist magazine.

"Are you sure you want to go to Bristol? I'm sure you could buy a barometer in London."

"It's got to be antique," they said.

"I'm sure you could get an antique barometer in London."

"These people are specialists," they said. "They deal with nothing else."

137

Who was I to argue? I took them to Bristol. They bought their barometer and haggled over the last few pounds, and then paid me handsomely for taking them there. The journey made their barometer very expensive indeed.

But now I remembered that shop. Wendy's brother lived in Bristol. So when she pressed me to tell her when we would have our barometer fixed I said, "The next time we go to Bristol to see Tony and Liz. There is a specialist barometer shop there."

That could have been months away. I went back to my book. But Wendy went to the telephone. Minutes later she was back. "Tony wants to know where the barometer shop is."

I don't know. Never a moment's peace. I put my book down and went to the phone and told him. He knew the place but he couldn't picture the shop.

Trust Tony. I ought to have known. He went to have a look, didn't he, and he found out about the shop, didn't he, and it was gone, wasn't it, so the question came again, "What are you going to do about the barometer?"

I gave up. There would be no peace until I had sorted the problem out. I hunted through Yellow Pages and sure enough, there was a place not too far away that saw to barometers. So we drove there and Wendy was happy. I took the barometer into the shop and I believed that at last my troubles were over.

"I'm sorry, sir, we don't deal with that kind of barometer."

That kind of barometer? I didn't know there was more than one kind. I thought a barometer was a barometer and that was that. Apparently ours was an aneroid barometer, whatever that is.

"Do you know anyone who does?" I asked.

"There aren't many people about who deal with barometers at all," he said.

I knew that was true. His was the only place in our Yellow Pages.

"There used to be a place in Bristol," he said.

I could have crowned him but I kept my cool. "It isn't there any longer." I said.

"Well I don't know anywhere else, I'm afraid. You could try London."

I thanked him politely and returned to the car in despair. I didn't want to have to go to London, but when Wendy has a bee in her bonnet she's like a dog with a bone. I knew she wouldn't let up until that barometer was fixed.

That night the phone rang. It was Liz, Tony's wife. "Tony's been doing a bit of research," she said. "There's a place in North Devon that specialises in barometers." She gave us the address and phone number, and under pressure from Wendy I phoned the very next morning. After all, North Devon was a darned sight better than London.

Yes, they dealt with aneroid barometers. Yes, they would be glad to look at ours but they were very busy. It would take them about three months to get it done.

Early that December we took our barometer to North Devon.

But whereas when I was driving Iris we travelled to and fro in a beautiful Jaguar 4.2, sleek and smooth and wonderfully comfortable, now we were driving a tiny little bouncy castle of a Daihatsu camper van.

26

A Trip to North Devon

I used to know that part of North Devon quite well. I did a lot of my growing up down there, although Wendy reckons I never did grow up. It was probably that, plus a desire to try out our new camper, that led me to suggest staying overnight. Normally we wouldn't think of camping so far into the winter. After all, ours was a very tiny camper. Staying overnight at that time of year was daft but I managed to persuade Wendy that we should.

We chugged across to Merton to 'Barometer World'. It's incredible. Merton is a small village right in the middle of nowhere, between Okehampton and Great Torrington. And hidden away off the main road there is what is perhaps the best barometer museum in the country, perhaps in the world. It's amazing.

We took our aneroid barometer there and yes, they could certainly repair and renovate it. They told us how long it would take and they gave us a price.

I think perhaps I've given the impression that Wendy was very keen to have that barometer renovated. Suddenly her enthusiasm died a death when she heard what it would cost. But it was too late. By now I was thoroughly hooked. We wandered round the museum to give us time to consider the matter.

"We can't afford it," she said. I ask you. When did that ever stop us doing anything? "We really can't afford it. Don't forget that we've only our pensions to rely on now."

That wasn't quite true. I was already beginning to earn celebrant's fees again. But she was probably right. We couldn't afford it. There was absolutely no way we could afford it. I had to recognise the fact. When you become a pensioner your income is fixed. It has no elasticity. No, she was quite right. We couldn't afford it. So we asked the man at Barometer World to go ahead. And then we drove on to Hartland and parked for the night close to Hartland Point. The sun smiled on us and we walked along the cliffs and enjoyed the sight of the sea churning away at the rocks below. Supper and bed in our snug little camper, and then the weather took over. It threw everything at us that night: rain, wind, hail, thunder, lightning, everything.

But our camper was facing into the wind, and though she rocked pretty violently we were as snug as two little bugs. We even managed to get some sleep. By morning the weather was so exhausted that it gave up and the sun came out again. We had breakfast, pulled down the roof, turned off the gas and set off for home.

"Are you going to show me something of Dartmoor on the way home?" Wendy asked.

Dartmoor? Why not? I know there are all sorts of strange tales about the things that can happen to you on Dartmoor and the presence of devils and suchlike, but I never gave these a thought. After all, the sun was shining.

141

And anyway, we would be on the northern fringes of the moor. There isn't all that much access by road. It would be nice and quiet.

So we drove happily past Okehampton to the A30 and then turned off onto a series of narrow roads through Sticklepath and past Throwleigh and Murchington to Chagford. More of the same brought us down to the B3212 and to Moretonhampstead. We were beginning to feel peckish by now. We crossed the A382 and took to the unclassified roads again to Doccombe and Dunsford. Just outside Dunsford we stopped for lunch.

There's a place that overlooks the River Teign. It's a lovely spot and we were just lucky. Another week or two and they would have closed for the winter. Unfortunately dogs were not allowed, so Becky had to stay in the car. That always made us hurry our lunch a little. We went back to the car and took her food and drink dishes out and put them in the car park. She wasn't very interested. She wanted a walk. So we set off for a walk in the woods, pushing her dishes under the car in case she was interested when we got back.

We were no sooner in the woods than the rain lashed down. We made that walk as short as we dared, fifteen to twenty minutes at most. And we were really racing when we got back to the car park.

Pip Squeak 2 wasn't there!

The two dog bowls stood in lonely state with the rain drowning Becky's food. She didn't seem to mind. She had found her appetite now so we had to wait while she finished her meal.

But Pip Squeak 2 wasn't there. It had taken a moment or two to register and then we hurried down to the restaurant and asked to use their phone. The police took all our details and promised to send someone. When he came the policeman asked to see where Pip Squeak had been parked.

"I can show you the exact spot," I laughed. "There are two dog bowls marking the place."

So we walked out to the car park. The two dog bowls weren't there! They simply weren't there. Now I can understand someone taking a car, but two dog bowls?

"Ah," said the policeman, "but this is Dartmoor, idn' it?" He seemed to think that this explained everything, and then he realised that because we were grockles – tourists, visitors, incomers – we might not understand. He explained that the fact is you can't explain. Not on Dartmoor you can't. Strange things happen on Dartmoor. We weren't all that interested. All we were interested in was how we were going to get home.

"Do you belong to any of the motoring organisations?" he asked.

"Yes, the RAC."

"Then I should give them a ring."

So we did. I gave the telephonist my name and membership number.

"Not you again."

"Yes, I'm afraid so."

"What is it this time? You've caught fire again? Or have you broken down? Let me guess. You've run out of petrol."

"Wrong," I said triumphantly. "Our car has been stolen."

"Stolen? Who on earth would want to steal *your* car?"

"What did you say?"

"I'm sorry, sir. I withdraw that last remark. What can we do for you?"

"We were rather hoping you could get us home."

So they sent us a taxi.

We hadn't been home long when the phone rang. It was the police. "We've found your car, sir. It's in Exeter and it's quite unharmed except for the lock on the driver's door."

"Oh wonderful. Thank you so much."

"We were wondering how the thieves managed to start it." I had been afraid someone would ask that question. "We left the spare keys in the glove compartment," I said.

There was a long pause and then he said, "I wouldn't do that again if I were you, sir."

"No."

"And it might be an idea to buy yourself a steering wheel lock, sir."

"Yes, I suppose it might." Although, I thought, there would be a key to that with the spare keys.

He must have read my mind. "And perhaps you'd like to consider fitting an immobiliser, sir."

"Aren't they terribly expensive?" And again I thought, 'and worked by a key with the spare keys.' Everything came down to those damn keys.

"Not too expensive, sir. It's cheaper than having your car stolen."

"Yes. Yes I see that. Do you think you'll catch the thieves?"

"I shouldn't think so, sir. My guess is that some lads were out on the moor and got caught in the bad weather. Your vehicle [he paused before he said 'vehicle' as if he didn't quite know how to describe it] offered them a nice, easy way to get back to Exeter free of charge. But it may have been a group of lads who target car parks on the moor. If it is, we're more likely to catch them."

Amazingly enough they did. The policeman told me what I had to do to collect my car, so all was well that ended well.

The following February we had to travel across to North Devon again to fetch the barometer from Merton. It wasn't exactly camping weather so we decided to do the round trip in one day.

We were thrilled with the barometer. It really did look splendid. And it worked! It always makes you feel good when you bring something lovely back from the dead. And it looked just right in the hall.

Wendy was delighted. I was pretty pleased myself. I'd been looking forward to being able to go to it each morning with a tap, tap, to check what it was reading and then to adjust it for the day. But Wendy always gets to it first. It's so galling. She's the one who goes tap, tap and then she comes to tell me whether it's gone up or down. It's not fair. I wanted to be the one to go tap, tap.

27

The Green Rover

I think that I've already mentioned that when our VW Weekender camper van came back to us we bade farewell to the Daihatsu. It had served us well but it was very tiny. In due course the Weekender was replaced by another camper van and then we decided that our camping days were over. . . although I still sometimes. . . NO, they really are over.

And so it was that we found ourselves with a small green Rover. You may remember that one of my first cars was Richard's Rover and that I loved them.

My Dad drove Rovers for years, the big heavy ones, Rover's last attempt at a luxury car. They seemed to fit my Dad perfectly, or he seemed to fit them, but he was a much bigger man than I am. I would have looked lost in them.

By the time we bought our green Rover the firm had gone, virtually the last survivor of a once magnificent British car industry – destroyed by bad management and greed. Whereas early Rovers were thought of as 'the poor man's Rolls' this last breed was more like 'the poor man's

Jaguar'. It had a sleek design and somebody once said to me, "The larger one is just about the most beautiful car on the road." It was certainly one of them and I found that I was very happy with our smaller one. She drove nicely and was very comfortable, a pleasure to drive and a pleasure to drive in.

We'd had a fair bit of use out of her, including holidays up in Surrey. And then we decided to travel north-east seeing some of the family en route. We stopped in Grantham for the night before going on to see a niece and her family. The following morning we did a bit of exploring and a bit of shopping and then we set off.

We stopped at red traffic lights and a few moments later there was a gentle bump. A young woman in a 4 by 4 had run into the back of us. There wasn't much damage – none at all to her vehicle. She took some photos of ours and we swapped insurance details and went on our way.

We visited my niece, rang our insurance company and agreed that we would deal with things when we got home, and then continued with our holiday. The holiday took us around the coast, with overnight stops until we reached Great Yarmouth.

There we took an attic room in an incredibly cheap hotel. The room had a broken window but it was overlooking the sea – perfect. And then a van drew up on the sea-front with its rear end facing our window. People opened up the back of the van and before long we found ourselves looking at a small stage. Crowds began to gather and then the stage began to fill with musical instruments and somebody was testing an amplifier.

Oh dear. What were we in for?

It turned out that we were in for some sort of gig but, as

it happened, we quite enjoyed their music and at round about half past ten they stopped so they didn't even stop us from enjoying a good night's sleep.

We carried on with our holiday and finally drove home, and our damaged Rover did us proud the whole time. Back at home we contacted the insurance company again and arranged for an assessor to come and look at the damage. And I went out to drive to town.

The car wouldn't start!

I've no idea why but having driven perfectly right through our holiday, she simply gave up the ghost.

The assessor came, looked at the little bit of damage to the rear of the car and wrote her off. I couldn't believe it and I'm sure that the young lady who had driven into us must have been equally astonished. The insurers sent a truck and carried her away and paid us promptly, and I went to a local garage and bought a Vauxhall. At the garage I told them what had happened and of my astonishment.

"Oh, they always write off Rovers," said the salesman.

A few weeks later he told me that he'd been on the internet and seen that our Rover had been sold for almost as much as the insurance company gave us!

That should have been the end of the matter but it wasn't. The young lady's insurance company refused to pay ours, and I can't say I blame them. It struck me that it would have been better if THEY had been the ones who had sent an assessor. Our car might well have been repaired but there would have been no argument. There were forms to fill in. There were phone calls. The whole thing dragged on for two years.

And we are still getting solicitors ringing up, "We hear that you have recently been involved in an accident. . ."

For goodness sake! Like any other cold caller, they get short shrift.

At this stage we were still driving two cars. Although I liked it, Wendy never really took to the Vauxhall. But she quite liked her little Renault Clio. The trouble was, it was only a two door car and when we dropped to one car we felt that we had to have a four door. I found another Renault, a Modus, but neither of us really took to it. The sit up and beg seating was very suitable for an antique and his wife but the car was a bit of a bouncy castle on the road. I began to take motoring magazines and to look around and Wendy began to take notice of what she saw on the television – and it was Wendy who saw what she wanted.

28

The Penultimate Chapter

My eldest son and I have sometimes talked about the environmental benefits of electric cars and the way that technology is making them viable.

And then he did a trip around Europe with someone in an electric car, a trip which led to a broadcast on BBC radio. It's the kind of mad thing he does. The poor chap has got a bit of his father in him I think – but he's a darned sight more adventurous.

I started looking at electric cars seriously but began to feel that they are still not sufficiently developed for us, either in terms of the miles they will do before being recharged or in terms of the national network of charging points.

It was Wendy who noticed that you can have the best of both worlds – a car that is both electric and petrol; a car that recharges itself! She was falling in love with the idea of a Toyota Auris hybrid.

Well, of course we could never afford one. That had been another snag with all-electric cars. They are still so new that by the time second-hand prices matched our pockets we'd be dead! So, sadly, there was no way that we could afford to buy Wendy's dream car.

And then I found one!

The salesman and I talked it through and then Wendy came with me and we went for a drive and tried it out and Wendy fell in love all over again.

It seems to have taken a long time, but when you've driven Jags for so many years nothing else is really good enough. Although she loved the VW camper too. But now, after so many false starts, at last she has found a car she's happy with.

And me? Yes, I like it too. I'm very impressed with it, delighted to get over 60 to the gallon, and find it a pleasure to drive. But although there have been cars I have liked more than others, on the whole I've always been content provided I had a car. After all, a car is a car is a car.

And yet. . . there really never has been anything quite like our Jags. And like Wendy, I loved the VW camper van too. You can't help hankering sometimes, can you?

However, I suspect that our Auris may well be the very last car we ever have – but on the other hand? Are there any more adventures still to come? I doubt it somehow. After all, we rarely venture far from home now. Work takes me twenty miles away and that's about our limit. But we did head off to Ilfracombe recently and the Auris passed the test with flying colours.

For years Wendy has been saying that she would like to go to Ilfracombe again. I think her memories go back to her teens when she cycled right round the north and south coasts of the south west from Bristol to Plymouth and back to Bristol on her fixed wheel bike. And then there were more recent memories, but still from way back, of her mother walking on Woolacombe beach wearing a fur coat and boots and of her son booting a ball into the wind and finding it return to him with interest.

I have my own memories going way back. When we were evacuees my father would come down by train to spend a weekend with us and he would take us for long walks to and along the coast. One of those walks took us from Croyde Bay right along the coast to Ilfracombe. When we finally got to the long stretch of sands that end at Woolacombe we couldn't walk on them. They were mined to protect us from invasion. So I had never actually been on Woolacombe beach.

And of course, when we got to Ilfracombe we never really saw the town (especially on the occasion when we lost my sister playing hide and seek and had a heck of a job finding her). We just caught the bus home.

The same was true later when I played cricket for a school team against Ilfracombe Grammar School. We just went to the school and came away.

So, because Wendy wanted to go there I booked a long weekend (although she'd had a long time to wait and wasn't too sure that she wanted to go anymore – WOMEN!).

We were at home walking on Burton Bradstock cliffs. "You won't find anything better than this," she said. We were walking at home up on the hills above Bothenhampton. "You won't find anything better than this," she said.

But we set off through the country lanes I love so much. "You won't find anything better than this," she said. And as we came out onto the main road to Taunton and then the Minehead road I did begin to wonder.

152

But we had a good meal and a short walk on the front in Minehead and Wendy began to enjoy herself, so I did too. And then we drove along to Lynmouth, climbing over Porlock hill and then running down Countisbury hill to the little harbour at the bottom. The Auris took Porlock hill in her stride and every other significant hill she met on the journeys of the weekend.

And of course, we remembered again the heroic story of the time when it was impossible to launch the lifeboat from Porlock so it was man-handled all the way over the hills to Lynmouth and launched from there – an incredible story of human determination and of stamina.

This whole area brought back memories for me. With my parents we walked up the valley to Watersmeet, jumping from boulder to boulder in the river and drinking pure, ice-cold water from a spring half way up.

And then, with a school friend, we cycled and camped on Exmoor. We cycled and walked all over, visiting the Doone Country. We left our bikes in a field above Watersmeet and walked down the valley to Lynmouth. We explored the village and Lynton above, and walked to the valley of rocks. And amazingly enough, by sheer fluke we met an aunt of mine who gave me ten bob (ten old shillings) which we blew on a meal. A week later the floods came down, doing all-told damage and killing something like thirty people. They changed the whole area for ever.

We have visited there since and I still love the area. On this trip we spent some time in Lynmouth and had another very pleasant walk before carrying on to Ilfracombe and out into the country where we were staying, on the side of a valley looking down on three lakes.

Over the long weekend we explored Ilfracombe itself and took a boat trip along the coast. It is an outstanding bit of coastline, as is most of the coast of Devon and Cornwall. Apart from fulmars nesting on the cliffs and the briefest glimpse of a school of porpoises and one solitary gannet, we saw very little sign of life, but it was a thoroughly enjoyable trip.

We walked on Woolacombe and Salcombe sands, but our favourite moments on the coast were at Lee, a tiny village with a footpath through fields and a valley to the sea. And inland, we meandered as I love to do, through country lanes. These have changed very little since my boyhood years. With spring starting late and a warm and sunny April, everything was coming out together. The hedges were full of primroses and when you walked you could see the violets too. And there were bluebells and whitebells and red campion (and by the coast sea campion and thrift), and there was masses of stitchwort about, a flower that rarely seems to be mentioned but which we both love.

I found that Wendy was no longer saying, "You won't find anything better than this." Perhaps the word 'better' is the wrong word to use. Ninety miles apart, West Dorset and North Devon are different worlds, both lovely and each of them with its own loveliness. A customer once asked me when we were driving through Richmond Park, "Which county do you reckon is the most beautiful?" In the end I couldn't answer him, I could only tell him of places that I love in a host of different counties.

There are changes, of course. There were no wind-farms when we were young. Much as we understand and believe in clean energy, we found them intrusive. I suppose that they have their own beauty and the occasional one or two have never bothered us but I hope that we can find other ways to produce clean energy, ways that do not deface the most beautiful and unspoiled countryside we have left.

When it was time to drive home we took a completely different route and travelled down the valley of the Exe through Dulverton and Exebridge. At that time of year this must surely be one of the most beautiful river valleys anywhere in the world.

"But you haven't said anything about Ilfracombe itself," said Wendy, when she read my screed. And of course, she's right. But how much did I tell you about London when I spent all those hours wearily waiting and walking in days gone by. And if I wrote about our twenty years in Bridport how much would I tell you about the town or its harbour at West Bay?

I'm not interested in towns and only rarely in architecture. Some of the boats in the harbour are beautiful enough to catch my eye but the things I love are the sea and the countryside and all our neighbours in the countryside, whether they be the cattle and sheep (or more recent introductions such as llamas) or the tiniest flower, ant, or beetle underneath our feet.

So this book has been about my love affair with cars, some of the people I have met or worked with, and the wide ranging and wonderful experiences of the British countryside that cars have enabled me to enjoy.

I've called this the penultimate chapter. The ultimate chapter can only be written when someone is dead and we aren't dead yet – not quite. But perhaps someone will take up the tale when I am in my electric wheelchair driving contentedly into oblivion.